PEACEKEEPERS

Irish Soldiers in the Lebanon

PEACEKEEPERS

Irish Soldiers in the Lebanon

Commandant Dan Harvey

MERLIN
PUBLISHING

Published in 2001 by

Merlin Publishing
16 Upper Pembroke Street
Dublin 2
Ireland

www.merlin-publishing.com

ISBN 1-903582-13-X

Harvey, Dan, 1959-
Peacekeepers: Irish Soldiers in the Lebanon
1. Ireland, Army 2. UNIFIL
I. Title
355.3'57'095692

Editorial Consultant: Roberta Reeners
Typeset by Artwerk Ltd, Dublin
Printed by Cox and Wyman Ltd, Reading

For Mary, Eva, Lynn and Mary Claire

CONTENTS

ACKNOWLEDGMENTS

Peacekeepers: Irish Soldiers in the Lebanon is a book which had to be written so that it might be appreciated that life and freedom are privileges which have a price. It is the soldier who often pays that price. Peace also has a price, and it is the peacekeeper who has to pay.

With advances in technology, transport and urbanisation, modern war impinges more and more cruelly on civilian populations. Irish soldiers serving the noble cause of peace now finds themselves performing humanitarian tasks as part of their varied peacekeeping role. Irish soldiers are highly regarded by the contributing UN member states and by the local populations in the many mission areas in which they have served. Unfortunately, the areas where peacekeeping missions are established have an inherent potential for violence and conflict. Irish peacekeepers appreciate that confrontations are faced, not by superior weaponry, greater firepower, better doctrine, new technology and superior mobility but by service men and women. Loyalty is the cornerstone of the soldier as peacekeeper, teamwork the essential ingredient, with camaraderie and courage the natural consequences.

In this personal account of one such peacekeeping tour of duty, I am attempting to contribute to a better understanding of both peacekeeping and peacekeepers. Here, it is the camaraderie and courage of my colleagues of all ranks — serving, retired and deceased — which I wish to acknowledge, along with their goodwill, encouragement and assistance in writing this book, the first of its kind.

Sincere thanks are offered to Brigadier General David Taylor, Colonel Desmond Travers, Lieutenant Colonel Padraigh O'Callaghan, Commandants Peter Young (deceased), Victor Laing and Pat Brennan (Military Archives), Commandant Eoghan O Neachtain (Retd), Captain Tom Clonan (Retd, Defence Forces Press Office), Michael Hartnett (Retd), Jim Long, and Jerry O'Leary, Captains Pat Winters (Retd), Billy Timmons (Retd), TD, Cillian Mc Domhnaill (Retd), Martin Reily (Retd), Denis Killian (Retd), Sean O'Keeffe, Jim Rea (Retd), and Michael McGinley (Retd), Sergeant Paddy Cremin (Retd), members of No. 5 Platoon, B Company, 56th Irish Battalion, and the many others whom I interviewed and who otherwise shared their memories, accounts and impressions.

Not least, sincere thanks to my family, as it is our families who make so many sacrifices in the support of our peacekeeping role.

GLOSSARY

AEs:	Armed Elements, a title for resistance groups, Lebanese or Palestinian, opposed to Israel
Amal:	Lebanese Shia Muslim militia and political group
AO:	Area of Operations
APC:	Armoured Personnel Carrier
BMR:	Battalion Mobile Reserve. Reinforcement unit used to assist companies in response to incidents
DFF:	De Facto Forces, or the South Lebanon Army (SLA), a pro-Israeli militia, chiefly Christian, led by General Haddad
IDF:	Israeli Defence Forces
Irish Batt:	Acronym for the Irish Battalion
LAUIs:	Locals Armed and Uniformed by the Israelis
Mossad:	Israeli Intelligence Agency
OGL:	Observer Group Lebanon. Unarmed UN observers established in Lebanon in June 1958
PLO:	Palestinian Liberation Organisation
Shin Bet:	Israel's Intelligence Agency
SLA:	Southern Lebanese Army. Pro-Israeli militia
UN:	United Nations
UNIFIL:	United Nations Interim Force in Lebanon

THE MIDDLE EAST

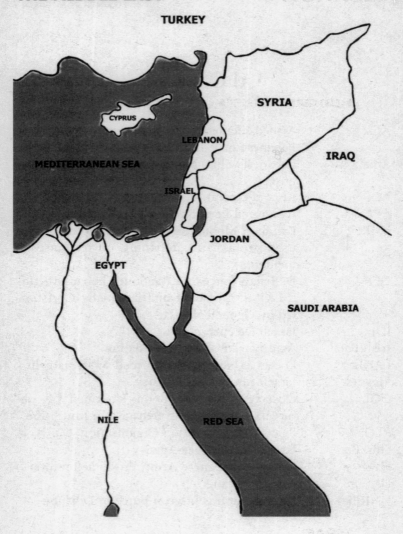

LEBANON

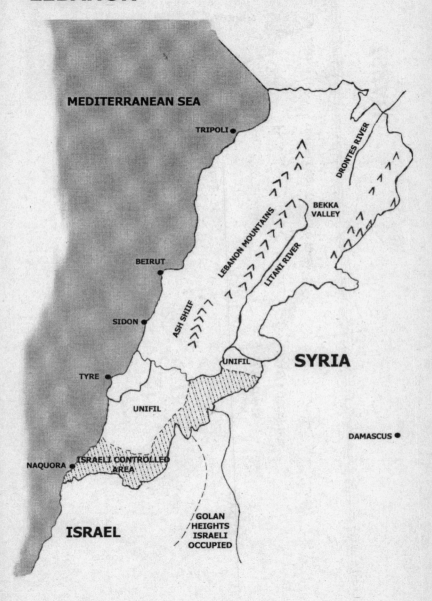

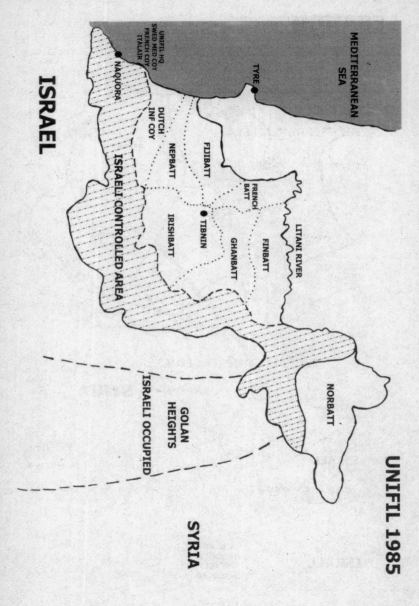

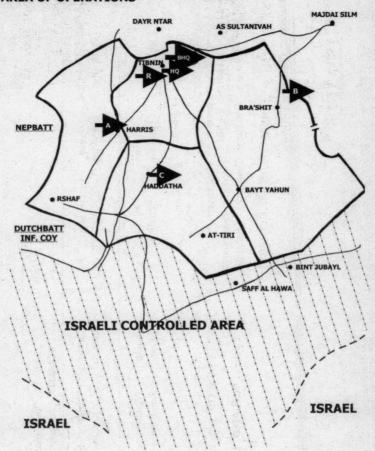

1985: IRISH BATTALION AREA OF OPERATIONS

ORGANISATION OF UNITED NATIONS INTERIM FORCE IN LEBANON (1985)

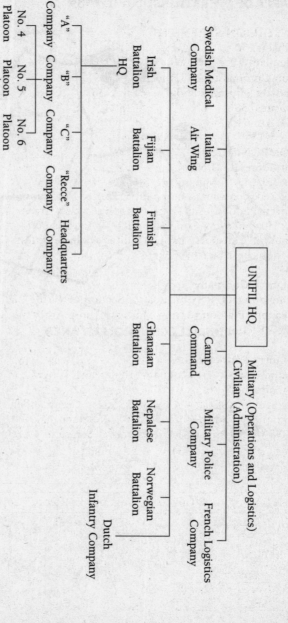

ORGANISATION OF IRISH BATTALION
UNIFIL 1985

BATTALION STRENGTH
Officers: 50
Chaplains: 2
Non-Commissioned Officers
(mostly Sergeants and Corporals): 207
Privates: 386
TOTAL: 645

COMPONENTS
Battalion HQ (BN)
3 x Infantry Company (A, B, C)
1 x Reconnaissance Company ("Recce" Company) — Heavy
Mortar Platoon, Anti-Tank Platoon, Cavalry Troop, Workshop
1 x Headquarters Company (HQ) — Signals Platoon, Engineer
Platoon, Transport Platoon, Military Police Section, Ordnance
Section, Pipe Band, Cooks

Infantry Company (Coy)
Company HQ, Reconnaissance Section, 2 x Rifle Platoons, 1 x
Weapons Platoon (81mm Mortar Section, Anti-tank Section, .5
HMG Section)

Infantry Platoon (PLN)
Platoon HQ — 1 Lieutenant, 1 Sergeant, 1 Private Driver, 1 Private
Signalman
3 x Section (SEC) — Corporal Section Commander, Corporal
Section Second-in-Command, 8 x Riflemen
(TOTAL: 26 Privates, 6 Corporals, 1 Sergeant, 1 Lieutenant)

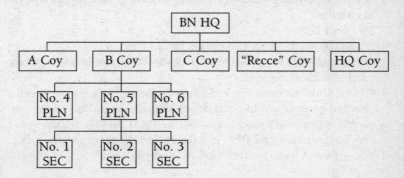

CHRONOLOGY

1939 – 45 — World War II and Nazi Holocaust

1948 — State of Israel set up in Palestine
  Over 110,000 Palestinian refugees arrive in Lebanon
  Rise of PLO
  Arab-Israeli War

1956 – 58 — Period of Pan-Arabism (Suez Crisis)

1967 — Six-Day Arab-Israeli War

1969 — Cairo Accord: Gave Palestinians certain legal rights in Lebanon

1970 — "Black September"
  Expulsion of Palestinians from Jordan created further influx of Palestinians into Lebanon.
  Creation of "A State within a State"
  Palestinian raids into Northern Israel from Lebanon

1973 — October Arab-Israeli War

1975 — Civil War in Lebanon (Muslim vs Christian), with Palestinian involvement

1976 — To prevent a Palestinian victory, Syrian troops intervene in Lebanese civil war.

1978 — "Operation Litani": Israeli invasion of Southern Lebanon
  Creation of pro-Israeli South Lebanese Army (SLA) under Major Saad Haddad
  Creation of Israeli-controlled "Free Lebanon"
  Withdrawal of IDF (Israeli Defence Forces)
  Irish Battalion arrives in Lebanon

1980 — Palestinian guerrilla raids into Northern Israel continue

1982 — "Operation Peace for Galilee": Second Israeli Invasion of Lebanon
  Siege of Beirut
  Evacuation of Palestinian militia from Lebanon
  Christian militia massacre of Palestinian dependants in Sabra and Shatilla refugee camps

1983 — Multi-national force deploys in Beirut to support Israeli-backed government but withdraws after deaths of US and French soldiers in massive suicide car bombs. AMAL and Hezbullah fighters harass Israeli and DFF/SLA forces, forcing them southwards.

1985 — Partial Israeli withdrawal to "security zone"

The IDF enlarges its controlled area of Southern Lebanon into a "Security Zone". This area overlaps with the UN area, and the Irish Battalion area in particular.

Tripartite Agreement

1988 — UNIFIL awarded Nobel Peace Prize

1991 — Syrian-Lebanese "Treaty of Brotherhood, Co-operation and Co-ordination". Syrian-Lebanese Pact of Defence and Security.

1992 – 95 — Hezbullah attacks into Israeli "security zone" of Southern Lebanon and Northern Israel

1996 — Israeli offensive in Lebanon (April Conflict: "Operation Grapes of Wrath")

Prolonged aerial, naval and land bombardment of Beirut, Tyre, Baalbek and Southern Lebanon to limit continuing Hezbullah attacks and pressurise Lebanese and Syrian governments to curb Hezbullah

Qana Massacre: Israeli artillery shells kill over 100 Lebanese civilians who were sheltering in the area of UNIFIL's Fijian battalion HQ

Palestinian-Israeli unrest: Construction of Jewish settlements in West Bank cause tensions to rise.

2000 — IDF withdraws from Southern Lebanon

2001 — Irish Batt withdraws from UNIFIL after 23 years, during which 44 Irish peacekeepers lost their lives; 1 remains missing

NOTE

Since 1978, UNIFIL operations were divided into three different phases:

- 1978 – 82 — Limit conflict between PLO and Israel
- 1982 – 85 — Extend protection and humanitarian assistance to Lebanese villagers under Israeli occupation, with the Israelis' partial withdrawal
- 1985 – 2000 — Contend with the conflicts generated by the continuing Israeli presence on Lebanese territory by preventing hostilities in the area and maintaining a measure of stability in Southern Lebanon

MEMORIAL LIST

Irish soldiers who lost their lives while serving with United Nations peacekeeping forces in Lebanon

Private Gerard Moon — Traffic Accident 1978

Corporal Thomas Reynolds — Traffic Accident 1978

Private Philip Grogan — Drowning Accident 1979

Private Stephen Griffin — Killed in action at battle of At-Tiri 1980

Private Thomas Barrett — Killed in action. Murdered by Major Haddad's militia 1980

Private Derek Smallhorne — Killed in action. Murdered by Major Haddad's militia 1980

Sergeant Edward Yates — Traffic Accident 1980

Corporal Vincent Duffy — Traffic Accident 1980

Private John Marshall — Natural causes 1980

Sergeant James Martin — Natural causes 1981

Private Hugh Doherty — Killed in action 1981

Private Kevin Joyce — Missing. Kidnapped by unknown armed elements 1981

Private Niall Byrne — Traffic Accident 1981

Private Gerard Hodges — Fire Accident 1982

Private Peter Burke — Killed in action at Tibnin Bridge 1982

Corporal Gregory Morrow — Killed in action at Tibnin Bridge 1982

Private Thomas Murphy — Killed in action at Tibnin Bridge 1982

Corporal George Murray — Accidental shooting 1984

Trooper Paul Fogarty — Traffic accident 1986

Lieutenant Angus Murphy — Killed in action by bomb planted by "Believers Resistance" 1986

Private William O'Brien — Killed in action 1987

Corporal Dermot McLoughlin — Killed in action 1987

Regimental Sergeant Major John Fitzgerald — Accidental shooting 1987

Corporal George Bolger — Natural causes 1987

Gunner Paul Cullen — Accidental fall from apartment block in Limassol, Cyprus 1988

Private Patrick Wright — Accidental shooting 1988

Private Michael McNella — Killed in action. Shot by Haddad's militia, Haddathah Compound 1989

Corporal Fintan Heneghan — Killed in action. Landmine explosion, Bra'shit 1989

Private Mannix Armstrong — Killed in action. Landmine explosion, Bra'shit 1989

Private Thomas Walsh — Killed in action. Landmine explosion, Bra'shit 1989

Sergeant Charles Forrester — Natural causes 1989

Commandant Michael O'Hanlon — Accidental shooting 1989

Corporal Michael McCarthy — Killed in action. Shot by DFF militia at At-Tiri 1991

Corporal Peter Ward — Killed in action. Shot at Al-Journ by Hezbullah 1992

Corporal Martin Tynan — Natural causes 1992

CQMS Declan Stokes — Natural causes 1993

A/Man Stephen O'Connor — Accidental shooting 1993

Sergeant John Lynch — Helicopter crash 1997

Private Kevin Barrett — Accidental shooting 1999

Private Billy Kidian — Mortar attack 1999

Trooper Jonathan Campbell — Motorcycle accident 1999

Private Declan Deere — Traffic accident 2000

Private John Murphy — Traffic accident 2000

Private Matthew Lawlor — Traffic accident 2000

Private Brendan Fitzpatrick — Traffic accident 2000

FOREWORD

At the time of writing this, the Irish Battalion serving with the United Nations in South Lebanon is packing up its equipment in preparation for its final withdrawal. Posts on rocky Lebanese hills which have been held at the cost of Irish lives have been dismantled. The last medal parade will take place on 26 September 2001. By October, the continuity of twenty-three years' service by the garrison of some 600 soldiers will end when the rear-guard drives up the coast to Beirut airport and is brought home on an Aer Lingus Airbus.

The Irish withdrawal is part of the reduction of the overall UNIFIL (United Nations Interim Force in Lebanon) force. This is taking place because of the Israeli government's decision in May 2000 to unilaterally withdraw its army from the buffer zone inside Lebanon along its northern border. The withdrawal followed a bloody conflict with the Lebanese Amal and, later, Hezbullah guerrilla forces. The Hezbullah's military wing, Islamic Resistance, had become increasingly efficient at attacking the Israeli Defence Forces (IDF) and its local surrogate militia, the South Lebanon Army (SLA). The increasingly deadly Hezbullah actions on the IDF fortresses dotted along the buffer zone in the late 1990s created pressure within Israel for a withdrawal. That was finally agreed to under the leadership of Israeli Prime Minister, Ehud Barak, who is also a former Chief of Staff of the IDF.

The withdrawal from Lebanon was a politically risky move for Barak's government. But it took place alongside the peace agreement with the Palestinian leadership of Yasser Arafat and amid hopes for a permanent peace settlement in the Middle East. Barak, one of the most decorated soldiers in the Israeli military, knew personally of the horror and tragedy in Lebanon. He had served in the thick of the Israeli invasion and bloody warfare of the early 1980s. Then, the IDF had swept past UNIFIL and Irish troops to capture virtually all of Lebanon and expel the Palestinian Liberation Organisation (PLO) that had been using South Lebanon as a base to launch attacks into Israel. Gradually, after the invasion, the Israelis withdrew to their border "security zone" some 10 kilometres deep along the border.

The UN Security Council in New York passed resolutions calling for a complete Israeli withdrawal. Israel, until Barak, ignored the resolutions and the security zone remained in place for more than fifteen years. In the centre of it, and often in the thick of artillery exchanges and bombing, stood the Irish Battalion. Typically, Hezbullah or Amal would launch surprise attacks on Israeli or SLA positions and withdraw quickly into the deeply ravined South Lebanese plateau. The Israelis and SLA would then respond with artillery barrages and aerial bombing.

My passport tells me that I have visited the area six times since the 1980s. On two occasions, Hezbullah attacks on northern Israeli towns had precipitated massive bombardments of the South Lebanese countryside, causing the flight of up to 300,000 people away from the havoc. On the first of these bombardments, known to the IDF as "Operation Accountability", I travelled to South Lebanon expecting to find a distressed and beleaguered battalion. Instead, under the command of Lieutenant Colonel Johnny Martin (now Brigadier General in charge of Western Brigade), I found a well ordered and, surprisingly, happy group of soldiers relieved not to have suffered any fatalities. With the lifting of the barrage, the troops were preparing for the visit of the then junior Defence Minister, Mr Noel Dempsey.

Mr Dempsey was the first foreign government minister to visit the area and the first to fly into Beirut airport since the ending of the civil war. The airport terminal was in bad order, still pockmarked with shell and shrapnel marks. He was whisked at alarming speed in an ageing American sedan across the apron to meet dignitaries and a Lebanese army guard of honour. He carried out his inspection with impressive decorum despite the flurry of activity around him by heavily armed bodyguards of the Lebanese leaders, and the oppressive humidity. He was then hurtled back across the airport apron in the battered sedan to where two Italian-crewed UN helicopters were waiting to take him to the UNIFIL headquarters 60 kilometres down the coast in Naquora. The helicopters swung far out into the Mediterranean to avoid fire from shore before beginning their descent into the UN camp of white portable cabins. After a night there, he travelled again by helicopter the further 40 kilometres inland to the Irish Battalion to be greeted by Lieutenant Colonel Martin on the hilltop helipad beside the Irish Battalion HQ in Tibnin. The minister toured the Irish outposts the following day and chatted amiably with the soldiers from home. Some of the posts had taken direct artillery hits from the Israeli side. Everywhere he found relieved and slightly dazed soldiers. Many had spent a week or more in the confines of bunkers to protect them from the shelling. All around, the countryside bore the marks of ten days of pulverising bombardment by the IDF artillery and F16 jets. The Israelis, despite their public denials, had fired phosphorous shells into South Lebanon. These horrifying weapons throw up a cloud of poisonous gas on impact and shower the surrounding area with stuff like napalm that burns through human flesh. The journalist and author, Robert Fisk, wrote about his experiences with this weapon in his book on Lebanon, *Pity the Nation*. He recounted how a victim had burst into flames in a hospital ward as the phosphorous continued to burn inside her flesh. A young boy had been struck in the groin by a piece of this material and lay in agony in hospital as it continued to burn deep into his body. Such was Lebanon at the time.

That night, Mr Dempsey was guest at a dinner in his honour at the Irish Battalion HQ. Irish troops strictly observe the maxim that an army travels on its stomach and, compared with the Spartan "international" diet at the UNIFIL HQ in Naquora, the food at Tibnin was tasty and filling. And while tributes were paid to all the battalion for their bravery and forebearance, the compliments to the army cooks prompted the biggest appreciation of the evening. Afterwards, there were drinks in the messes which continued after the minister had retired to bed. The soldiers who had served through the ominous build-up and then the bombardment itself began to relax for the first time in many weeks. Most were friendly and grateful for the moment's respite.

The next day, Minister Dempsey was brought to meet the Tibnin *mukhtar* (mayor) and sipped sweet coffee with local elders who spoke through Hassan Fawaz, the Irish Batt interpreter, to tell him how greatly they appreciated the help and protection the Irish soldiers brought them. The minister visited the local orphanage which had been adopted as the battalion's pet charity. The waifs, who had endured the bombardment in the shelter of Irish bunkers, clung to his arms. There were tears in people's eyes as the ministerial convoy returned to Tibnin for the journey back to meet the newly formed Lebanese government in Beirut.

At one point in my visit, I found myself standing over a partly exploded phosphorous shell taking a photograph. During my stay, *The Irish Times* carried a cartoon by Martyn Turner depicting the Israeli bombardment with the image of a huge *Tyrannosaurus Rex*, wearing a helmet with the Star of David, stomping over miniature civilians. The caption, referring to the then Hollywood box-office hit, *Jurassic Park*, read: "Jew-rassic Park'. This cartoon was syndicated to newspapers around the world. The Israeli government responded with a furious diplomatic and political attack on the Dublin newspaper which had published the image. Days after returning home from the war zone, I was quickly sent back to Israel where there were tense meetings with senior government figures. One meeting led to the Deputy Minister for Defence, Mr Mordechai Gur, shouting back at me as he was pressed on the Israeli use of phosphorous shells.

I again visited the Irish Battalion in 1996 during another Israeli bombardment known as "Operation Grapes of Wrath". This time, Israeli airburst shells hit the headquarters in the village of Qana (also spelt Cana, it is the scene of the Bible's marriage feast) of the adjoining UN battalion area controlled by Fijian troops. The Fijians were sheltering hundreds of civilians, mostly women and children, who had been unable to flee the bombardment. The shells, bursting about 30 metres above the camp, showered the refugees with lacerating shrapnel, slicing through the pitiable humans beneath. Many of the dead were decapitated or eviscerated. Doctors and medics from the Irish Batt HQ rushed to help amid this carnage. Some 106 people, mostly women and children, were killed.

Again on this occasion, an Irish minister travelled to South Lebanon. The Minister for Defence, Mr Sean Barrett, was the only foreign government figure to visit the devastated area in the aftermath of the bombardment. He even arrived before any member of the government in Beirut. He toured the Irish positions and observed the devastation wrought by "Operation Grapes of Wrath". The deaths of so many women and babies traumatised the returning Lebanese. And, during Mr Barrett's visit to the scene of the slaughter in Qana, a running gun battle broke out between local Hezbullah and Amal fighters in the streets just yards away. The party sprinted for shelter.

Later, after the minister left, I went with the army's Press Officer, Commandant Eoghan O Neachtain, to the huge funeral service for the dead infants and mothers at the Hippodrome in Tyre, the same place where Roman games were once held and where another Hollywood movie, *Ben Hur*, was filmed on location.

My last visit was just as the Israelis withdrew, suddenly and with little bloodshed, after an intense campaign of harassment by an increasingly deadly and sophisticated Islamic Resistance onslaught. In the following days, a new peace returned to the area. There was no shooting or bombing. Hezbullah had pre-negotiated the return of the Lebanese displaced from the

Israeli security zone. I met elderly men and women returning
to their villages and homes for the first time in more than
twenty years. In many cases, they were accompanied by
excited grandchildren who had grown up in Beirut or abroad
and had never seen their precious ancestral homes. At the
village of At-Tiri, where four Irish soldiers had died protecting
besieged Muslim villagers against marauding Christians from
the SLA, I sat down with the *mukhtar* and local Hezbullah
leaders. They told me of their appreciation of the Irish sacrifice
for their people. They would erect a plaque in the village for
the Irish soldiers who had died. Outside, the noise of
children's laughter filled the narrow streets, streets which had
been empty and silent except for the sound of shelling and
bombing for two decades. The few old people who had stayed
were fed and protected by Irish soldiers who clung on despite
repeated attack and harassment.

Elsewhere, accompanied by Commandant Joe McDonagh
and Commandant (now Lieutenant Colonel) Declan Carberry,
I met newly arriving Muslims camped on a barren hillside that
was once a village surrounded by orchards and olive groves but
which had been blown apart and bulldozed by Christian
neighbours and Israelis. The Muslims, some of whom had
come from the United States in anticipation of the IDF
withdrawal, vowed to rebuild their homes. The local Christians
who had fought with the Israelis were clearly in a state of
nervousness but nowhere was there any sign of retribution.

As the Lebanese Muslims began to move back into their
homeland, it began to become clear that UNIFIL and the Irish
troops had, at last, achieved their purpose. We attended the
Hezbullah's dramatic victory rally in the "liberated" town of
Bint Jubayal, complete with sacrificial sheep to welcome the
arrival of their leader, Sheikh Nazrallah. Then on to Beirut for
the flight home from the sparkling new marble and glass
airport.

Since my first visit, the shattered heart of the city has been
massively rebuilt. The South, too, has been rebuilt. Returning
Lebanese, some of whom have made fortunes and become

merchant princes, have built beautiful palaces on the hillsides where there were once shell-pocked skeletons of houses.

In just over two weeks' time, the final withdrawal of Irish troops begins. The battalion headquarters, as always intended by the UN, is to be handed over to the Lebanese army. However, while Lebanon is finally at peace, the wider picture in the region has taken another turn for the worse. The peace negotiated between the Israelis and Palestinians across the border has broken and strains between Israel and its neighbours are again beginning to show. The towns and countryside where the Irish once served, however, remain at peace for now.

Jim Cusack
Security Editor, *The Irish Times*
7 September 2001

IRON FIST

Early February 1985

Not yet dawn, the first rays of the Mediterranean sun would soon gently kiss the tiny Shia Muslim settlement laying peacefully in the folds of rock on the scrub-covered hillside. A pretty village, it was situated south of Lebanon's Litani River, east of the historic sea port of Tyre. Old vines and trees rambled amidst the spectrum of dull greys, grey-browns and mud-browns of the one and two-storey flat-roofed, breeze-block houses. Tiny alleyways, once paved, fed into narrow streets which led past the school and mosque into the village square and community waterhole.

This picturesque mountain hamlet was home to a rural community who made their living in the nearby stony waddies in the traditional way: tending their sheep and goats and raising crops of citrus and soft fruit, olives and vegetables. They were close to the land and bore all of its joys, vagaries and hardships.

The unsettled herds of goats and sheep were the first to alert the rangy village dogs that something was amiss. Unknown to the sleeping inhabitants, their peaceful lives were about to be brutally and shockingly shattered.

In Phase One, Israeli troops sealed off all access routes to the village before the search operation commenced. Army foot patrols silently positioned themselves to close off the more inaccessible paths and likely avenues of escape. Now, their "M113s", or as they themselves liked to call them, their Zelda armoured personnel carriers, prepared to block off the roads and tracks. The village would soon be sealed off, with all entry and exit points covered by troops in fire positions. Anyone trying to make a run for it would be shot. The Israeli occupation of South Lebanon was becoming increasingly repressive as their army began to execute its "Iron Fist" policy against the Lebanese guerrilla fighters.

In Phase Two, Israeli forces moved into the village with some 200 personnel in twenty armoured personnel carriers as snipers took up key positions. This sudden, violent, shock arrival of large numbers of Israelis caused utter horror amongst the villagers, overwhelming them with noise and chaos. Children shrieked in terror while clinging fiercely to their mothers. Hysterical women made hopeless efforts to defend their menfolk. With orders shouted, constant screaming, dogs barking wildly, warning shots fired, the once-tranquil village erupted in pandemonium.

A headquarters was established in the village school and a loudspeaker jeep instructed all males, including youths and older men, to present themselves at this holding centre. The male population was then divided into three groups: youths, men and old men. Anyone who was considered suspect was separated from the rest, bound with plastic locks, shoes either unlaced or removed, and then blindfolded. They were lined up, heads against the wall, and surrounded by a cage of barbed wire. One party of troops provided outer security while another covered the prisoners. Throughout the morning and early afternoon, suspects were interrogated individually; villagers were required to identify suspects from photographs. Simultaneously, sections of up to ten Israeli soldiers searched specific houses and areas. Spray paint was used to mark those buildings which were clear and those in which weapons and ammunition were allegedly found. These were then blown up. The searches were thorough and systematic.

As the operation was wound down, some of the older and younger men were released and the M113 armoured personnel carriers moved position to secure an orderly withdrawal. A security party took up position around the holding centre to cover the prisoners and secure the rear. Armoured personnel carriers were brought up, and the suspects, still bound and blindfolded, were bundled inside.

Phase Three was critical because tensions were quite high. The male population had been confined for about eight hours without food or water while the women and children had worked themselves into hysteria. The Israeli soldiers were quite nervous, particularly of the hysterical women, indicating that they would shoot if the women came too close. A helicopter searched the area for other would-be attackers and a ground reconnaissance party moved out at the head of the main convoy. As they advanced, they fired into areas thought likely to conceal ambushers. The last group to depart was the rear security party. They made a hasty retreat.

On this occasion, no deaths resulted — it would not always be so.

During February 1985, Israeli defence forces mounted eight cordon-and-search operations, seven in the French UN battalion area and one in the Finnish. The Irish battalion, on high alert to curb such activities, was also destined for conflict with the Israelis.

Patience, Persistence, Persuasion

Sitting in the officers' mess at Collins Barracks in Cork and looking out at the early summer growth on the trees, I was unsettled. A mix of conflicting emotions rendered me ill at ease. To a greater or lesser degree, this uneasiness is felt by all who return from their peacekeeping duties in South Lebanon to the mainstream garrison existence at home. This sense of restlessness is all the more acute for those whose overseas tour had, through operational circumstances, been eventful. Three months previously, I had even thought I might not see this moment. Along with other members of my platoon, I had faced very real dangers, confrontations, fire fights and the risk of open warfare with the Israeli-backed South Lebanon army and other militia gangs hired by Israel to terrorise the population inside the UN zone.

Our platoon was one of three which made up B Company. Five companies, ABC headquarters and reconnaissance companies comprised the full Irish battalion. Six such battalions of differing nationalities, along with support units and headquarters' staff, constituted a peacekeeping force of nearly six thousand: the United Nations Interim Force in Lebanon — UNIFIL.

UNIFIL had come a long way from being "the right force in the right place at the right time". It had been asked to do an impossible job, without the proper resources, in the face of utterly ruthless and unscrupulous adversaries. In the last few months of our tour, the task facing UNIFIL was more difficult than anything seen up to then. We were caught in the middle of the shambles which the Israelis seemed determined to leave behind as they withdrew from Southern Lebanon. In more senses than one, UNIFIL — and the Irish battalion in particular — had been asked to take a leap in the dark as the Israeli army withdrew. We were at sea in uncharted waters, giving rise to some frightening and intense moments in which Irish peacekeepers were placed at increased risk. All manner of dangers lay in wait, especially at the hands of the highly volatile, ill-disciplined militia gangs. We had become the meat in the sandwich between Lebanese resistance fighters on one side and the Israeli-hired militiamen on the other as they set about enlarging their so-called security zone forward of that which already existed along a frontier inside Southern Lebanon. Unfortunately, this proposed new line coincided with portions of the Irish battalion area of the UN zone. The situation required a more tough-minded, robust response than the traditional peacekeeping *modus operandi* of patience, persistence, persuasion. The pro-Israeli militia gangs had not been slow to put their weapons to active use. Increasingly, shots were fired in anger and with more deadly intent. In order to keep the peace, we had to fight for it.

Both before and since the second Israeli invasion in 1982, Lebanon had become a place of violence and death: civilians, resistance fighters, Israeli soldiers, militiamen, Palestinians and peacekeepers, all had been among the dead and injured. There were thousands of casualties and fatalities, many thousands more displaced, missing, traumatised. Neither had the Irish battalions been immune from tragedy: over the years, Irish peacekeepers had experienced injury and death.

I was relieved to be home. I had enjoyed my month's leave to the full but still, I felt exhausted and somewhat haunted. This was not because of any disproportionate feelings of having abandoned the South Lebanese population of our area to their fate. Far from it: a new Irish battalion, dedicated and professional, had taken up the peacekeeping mantle. My feelings arose from the fact that I had sworn to myself that I was never going back. But now, in spite of everything my platoon and I had been through, I knew, if given the chance, I would go back. It was all a bit baffling, but as I was later to appreciate, it was neither uncommon nor unusual.

I was extremely proud of how our platoon had performed, yet I wondered if pride was appropriate, given the past and continuing horror of events in Lebanon. Having faced unfair criticism at home for years about our ability to defend our own shores against an invading army, I knew that our envied international reputation as peacekeepers was not only well-earned but hard-earned. We had played our part well and had not dishonoured the efforts and sacrifices of past Irish peacekeepers in holding a very stretched thin blue line intact at an uncertain time. It was a dangerous mission in which we had put our own lives in danger to save local people and prevent the conflict in our area from escalating further.

To appreciate fully the role of the Irish battalion with the United Nations Interim Force in Lebanon, it is necessary to understand the context within which it operated. Peacekeeping is a paradox: there is no mention of it in the UN charter. Rather, this role developed as a pragmatic response to the threats posed by regional conflicts after World War II. Born of necessity, it was developed by the UN as a practical response to conflicts which threatened world peace and security. The UN's peacekeeping role tried to create an atmosphere in which confidence-building and bridge-building allowed the diplomatic and political steps towards peace. It gave the superpowers an opportunity to stand back while UN observer missions or peacekeeping forces interposed themselves between hostile states, communities or nations, thus creating time for political initiatives.

Most commonly, peacekeeping has been used to supervise and maintain ceasefires, to assist in troop withdrawals and to provide buffer zones between opposing forces. Operationally, a peacekeeping mission is a relatively reactive operation which tries to de-escalate conflicts by peaceful means. Certain important principles are central to successful peacekeeping: the consent and co-operation of the parties involved in the conflict; the impartiality of the UN forces; and the non-use of force except in self-defence.

In 1958, shortly after becoming a member state of the UN, Ireland dispatched fifty officers to observer duties in Lebanon. In the summer of 1960, Ireland contributed a contingent to the UN force in the Congo. In March 1964, an Irish battalion was one of the first on the ground in Cyprus. Many tributes have since been paid to these first Irish peacekeepers, many of whom paid a high price.

* * *

A knowledge of the historical and contemporary events which led to the deployment of the peacekeeping force in a complex and difficult operational situation in Lebanon is important. Throughout the centuries following the destruction of Jerusalem in 70 AD, small numbers of Jews had lived in Arab-dominated Palestine, the former name for Israel. According to the censuses of 1922 and 1931, continuing waves of immigration had brought the Jewish population of Palestine to a sizeable minority. Following the Nazi's extermination of European Jews during the Holocaust, the aspiration emerged that Palestine would become the universal refuge of all Jews. On 14 May 1948, Israel was established as a Jewish homeland and proclaimed a separate state upon the termination of the British mandate for Palestine. Thus did a large part of Palestine became part of Israel, with more than 100,000 Palestinians becoming refugees. Dispossessed and displaced, they fled to neighbouring Lebanon and Jordan. Since 1948, the state of Israel has had a Jewish majority.

The proclamation of the Jewish state was followed by war between Israel and the neighbouring Arab states, ending in victory for Israel and the signing of separate armistice agreements. The old Palestinian boundaries with Lebanon and Syria on the north, and with Syria on the east, remained unchanged. In June 1967, following the Six-Day War with Egypt, Syria and Jordan, Israel occupied the Sinai Peninsula in

Egypt, the Gaza Strip, the West Bank of the Jordan River including the Old City of Jerusalem, and the Golan Heights region in south-western Syria. The expulsion of the militant Palestinians from Jordan in "Black September" 1970 caused yet another influx of Palestinians into Lebanon, creating "a state within a state".

Following raids by Palestinian guerrillas from Lebanon into Israel, the Lebanese themselves were affected by large-scale Israeli retaliatory raids. Weakened by a civil war of their own essentially between Muslim and Christian Arabs, the Lebanese made various failed attempts to control the Palestinians. Syrian forces had to intervene to prevent a Palestinian victory over the Muslim Lebanese, but later changed allegiance to support the Lebanese Christians and the Palestinians. Matters were further confused by an Israeli army invasion of the south of the country in 1978, launched to prevent Palestinian guerrilla incursions across the Lebanese border into Israel.

The United Nations' force of nearly 6,000, made up of contributing nations which included Ireland, was placed in Southern Lebanon to prevent war between the two parties — the Israelis and the displaced Arab Palestinians and, by extension, the Syrian military forces inside Lebanon. The UN's mandate was to confirm the withdrawal of the Israeli forces to the international border, restore peace and security, and assist the Lebanese government in ensuring the return of its effective authority in the area.

As a direct result of the Israeli army invasion, the arrival of the UN force began in March 1978. This had been triggered by a Palestinian attack on Israel in which more than thirty Israeli civilians had been killed, the most recent fatalities in the saga of revenge and retaliation taking place in both directions across the Lebanese border. "Operation Litani" forced the Palestinians to withdraw north of the Litani River and into the coastal city of Tyre, although they did not leave Lebanon completely. Israel itself made a partial withdrawal from South Lebanon but not before establishing an Israeli-controlled security zone immediately north of its border with Lebanon;

this became known as "the enclave". In the final phase of its withdrawal, the Israeli army transferred most of their positions near the enclave into the hands of Major Haddad's pro-Israeli Christian militia. The UN force was then deployed in its wake, in a configuration which remained largely unchanged after the withdrawal.

After the Israeli army's withdrawal, the Palestinian guerrillas regrouped. With much of their equipment intact, the situation in South Lebanon remained extremely tense and volatile. The UN force which had entered Lebanon to separate Israeli and Palestinian forces was often fired on by both sides. The Palestinians continued their actions against Israel until June 1982 when the Israeli Minister for Defence, Ariel Sharon, directed the Israeli army to mount "Operation Peace for Galilee", the second invasion of Lebanon. Its stated objective was the destruction of all Palestinian guerrilla bases in South Lebanon. Its less obvious purpose, however, called "Operation Snowball", had a twofold aim: to set up a right-wing pro-Israeli government in Beirut, and to break the will of the Palestinians in the West Bank by dispersing the PLO leadership. Although this full-scale invasion forced most of Arafat's Palestinian guerrillas out of Lebanon, it resulted in the Israeli army's prolonged military occupation of Lebanon.

Meanwhile in the south, along with Major Haddad's Christian militia, another pro-Israeli militia had been set up. Known as "locals armed and uniformed by the Israelis" (LAUIs), they were the latest in a string of Israeli-paid vigilantes — untrained and ill-disciplined gunmen, opportunists and criminals — who operated within the UN area and whose activities had such an adverse effect on the normal lives of the people, many of whom lived in fear of their very presence. In maintaining an impartial role, the Irish battalion had to cope with their intimidation and coercion which often resulted in tense stand-offs, difficult stalemates and dangerous confrontations.

This record tells that story.

CONCEPT OF OPERATIONS

0700 hrs. 03 September 1984. Platoon form-up commences
As I stood to attention on the square of Collins Barracks, waiting to inspect my platoon of twenty-six privates, six corporals and one sergeant, I felt dwarfed by the sheer size of my surroundings. The great space of four square acres, reputedly the largest in Europe, was enclosed on three sides by beautifully proportioned Georgian buildings. The length of each building ran to over two hundred yards and rose to just three stories. The plastered walls were set off by finely crafted windows surrounded by cut limestone. The scale and number of windows meant that the interiors were usually flooded with light and there was no feeling of claustrophobia as in other barracks and military posts.

Though late summer, the early-morning chill forced me to alternatively curl up and then extend my toes inside my boots as I gently swayed on the balls of my feet to keep the circulation going. As I did so, I mentally calculated the lengthy preparations involved in Phase One of the platoon's forming-up. For everyone, the checklist had been long. From the initial volunteering stage, through recommendation and on to selection, a process of interview, review and nomination was required. The home unit commander had to satisfy himself of each soldier's suitability for the mission and thus had to consider family circumstances, health, previous overseas reports, competency on the home unit front and domestic considerations. None of these could give any cause for doubt.

Immediately prior to the initial three-week forming-up period, the administrative process commenced — but not before a thorough medical examination which included x-rays, dental checks, blood-grouping and inoculations against yellow fever, polio, cholera, typhoid and hepatitis. The form-up would reinforce the platoon members' weapons-handling proficiency, with both day and night range practices with our personal small arms, FN rifles, Gustav submachine guns and Browning automatic pistols. Kit inspections determined what clothing and equipment had to be issued. Identification discs, photographs, documentation checks — including making out a will — were completed and double-checked. Only then did the three individual platoons in the Irish battalion advance to the company concentration where training commenced in earnest.

24 September 1984. Company form-up commences

Phase Two consisted of three weeks' hard grind in the barren, windswept humps and hollows of the 3,500 acres of Kilworth's military training area where every effort was made to simulate what lay ahead: six months of soldiering on a patch of mountainous Middle Eastern terrain. As the battalion never gets the chance to assemble for full manoeuvres before departure, the men of the other companies were being put through their paces in army training areas like the Curragh, the Glen of Imaal and Kilbride. The peacekeeping techniques which had been developed over the years in response to the ever-changing situation were detailed, explained and discussed again and again. In true army fashion, the standard operating procedures were rehearsed repeatedly, day and night, and included observing, patrolling, reporting, negotiating, monitoring, escorting and the correct conduct of checkpoints. The company's light mortars and anti-tank weapons were also fired by day and night, as was a "new arrival" into service, the Browning heavy machine gun (HMG/M2/0.5"). With its heavy barrel, the "point five" was an updated model of the 1930s design. Two million had been made initially and it remains one of the most powerful machine guns in existence. Irish troops encountered it or, more precisely, were subjected to its disruptive effect when it was used by the Israelis and their armed militias. It was introduced to provide a viable response to that self-same threat and was first used to that purpose during our tour. We also conducted long-range patrols, a route march and night compass marches. Through all this activity, the company's cohesion and *esprit de corps* were built up. Those less single-minded about going overseas were beginning to think twice about their decision.

09 October 1984. Officer briefing

Not having experienced a briefing of a similar scale, scope or seriousness, the heightened expectation was almost palpable. The day-long briefing of the officers of the newly formed, Lebanon-bound battalion concluded on a high note. This was particularly true for the "first-time" officers who nonetheless tried to contain their anticipation lest they betray their excitement.

The formal briefing presented the first opportunity for all battalion officers to assemble. Each was conscious of the necessity of assuming a new unit identity as the entire battalion had been drawn from different commands, corps and services. All were volunteers.

Each individual briefing officer addressed his subject comprehensively. Some had recently returned from overseas battalions, while others were from the appropriate sections of the defence forces. Their detailed exhibition of photographs showing platoon positions, checkpoints, observation posts and company headquarters seemed to catch the uninitiated off-guard, creating a sense of an exciting and potentially dangerous experience — a true adventure. The operational summary of recent routine incidents reinforced the strangeness of it all. The place names, personalities and procedures were a language all their own, foreign to anything remotely comparable at home.

The Irish were deployed as one of the participating countries which included Norway, Sweden, Finland, France, Italy, Holland, Fiji, Nepal and Ghana — all part of UNIFIL. With a total strength of nearly 6,000, the Irish contributed a force of approximately 700 which was made up of the battalion stationed in the hills of South Lebanon and the much smaller component at UNIFIL headquarters in Naquora on the coastal plain immediately north of the Israeli border.

Concluding the officer briefing, an operational summary identified two specific trouble spots within the Irish area of responsibility. Their potential for confrontation was highlighted, leaving the platoon commanders to wonder which of them would have to face this hostility. The prospect was all the more daunting because, at an early stage, the battalion commander had decided that the customary rotation of companies around the Irish battalion area was unlikely; they would remain fixed in their respective company areas throughout the tour. For this reason, the three infantry company commanders decided that platoon rotations within their own company areas would take place on a bi-monthly basis.

15 October 1984. Battalion activated

The activation date for the Lebanon-bound battalion saw fifty officers, two chaplains, 207 non-commissioned officers and 386 privates, a total of 645, established as an official reality. It was now a legal entity with its own identity. Two days later, the battalion assembled and paraded together, for the one and only time in its existence, in McKee Barracks, Dublin. The battalion flag was blessed by the defence forces' head chaplain and the troops were reviewed by the Minister for Defence. The completion of a six-month tour of duty in Lebanon was regarded as a coming of age for the junior officer and soldier alike, with the first trip overseas being a milestone in one's career.

"Don't be scared... be prepared" was a well-used catch phrase of the time; I was probably a bit of both. My time in the army had equipped me as well as could be expected, with my "domestic experiences" including operational service on the border, in Portlaoise Prison, and on various other internal security taskings around the country: cordons and searches, checkpoints, cash escorts, conventional warfare exercises of varying scales, specialised courses. All conditioned the young officer and soldier, complementing the more focused preparations for overseas. Fortunately, I knew most of my platoon well, having shared home service with them. Even before setting foot on the out-bound aircraft, our working relationship was already well established. They all understood that my main mission was to bring my thirty-three guys home alive.

*   *   *

For a soldier, going overseas is always an attraction. One can gain experience of an operational nature which cannot be acquired at home. Leadership skills can be evaluated and developed, and there is the opportunity to assess the Irish battalion's strengths and weaknesses vis-à-vis other nationalities and armies. For me, it was not only a professional work experience but also a life experience. I couldn't wait to settle in and appreciate those values which formed the military peacekeeping experience. I was anxious to learn how best to concentrate our efforts in preventing or limiting the hostilities, as well as providing humanitarian assistance amidst the internal divisions and turmoil: in short, to shield the long-suffering Lebanese from the worst effects of the persistent violence and conflict.

ROTATION

07 November 1984

Instrumentation check completed, clearance granted by Dublin airport air traffic control, the Aer Lingus Boeing 747 taxied onto runway two-four for take-off. On board were members of the third and final rotation, or "chalk", completing the battalion's airlift to Lebanon; Chalk One and Chalk Two had departed a fortnight and week previously. Done in three phases over two weeks, the rotation maintained continuity on the ground in the Irish battalion area and allowed the newly arriving battalion time to ease themselves in. The two-week handover involved briefings, reconnaissance, meeting contacts and the introduction of procedures and drills appropriate to the evolving situation in the area of operations.

My platoon and I, like the remainder of the chalk, were pleased to be airborne and Lebanon-bound, having experienced the unenviable wait associated with being listed on the final aeroplane manifest. As company logistics officer, I was responsible for ensuring that all the stores, equipment and personal luggage left the barracks by convoy and were loaded onto the aircraft. This involved being present at the two previous airlifts and witnessing the excitement of their departure, only to return to a state of suspended animation.

The roar of the aircraft's Pratt and Whitney engines on lift-off signified an end to our limbo as the Jumbo rose into the early morning sky, leaving Ireland cloaked in darkness. The mood on board the five-hour flight was convivial and relaxed. This type of charter was a special favourite among Aer Lingus cabin crews who volunteered to be rostered for them. Their passengers, all able-bodied, were noted for being undemanding and good-humoured. Some slept, the early hour taking its toil. Others pondered their moments of departure from loved ones. Most were mindful of their destination and the possibilities which lay ahead.

Five hours later, the thud of the landing gear announced our imminent arrival at Ben Gurion airport, Tel Aviv, Israel; Beirut airport was closed due to the turmoil resulting from the Israeli military occupation of Lebanon. Adjusting our watches two hours forward, we stepped out of the plane and were immediately struck by a blast of heat. Although still mid-morning, the temperature was already high, unimaginably so for an Irish November morning... but then, this certainly wasn't Ireland.

The scene on the airport tarmac was one of highly organised activity. The heavily tanned members of the homeward-bound Irish battalion were drawn up in file, delighted at the sight of the "big green bird" from home. There was an aura of ease about them arising from a sense of accomplishment, a subtle superiority that demanded and deserved our respect. We willingly bowed to their hard-gained experience and in truth were envious of it. I was mindful of how we were regarded by them and how, in turn, we would similarly regard our replacements... but much would occur before then.

No intermingling was allowed between those arriving and departing, but words of welcome, good-natured jeers and other shouts of encouragement were exchanged in abundance. The inevitable chorus of "Jingle Bells" was sung to impress upon us the season for which we had volunteered.

A large convoy of buses, trucks and jeeps from the French logistic contingent was efficiently marshalled into position by a mixture of Irish battalion military police, French movement control personnel and Israeli airport officials. We boarded our designated transport under the supervision of Irish battalion liaison officers drawn from companies which had arrived a fortnight previously.

There followed a slick subdivision of our chalk according to company deployment on the ground. Though well organised, the unloading of the plane took some time and late lunchtime saw us moving out of the airport proper. In so doing, we were crossing a threshold into a new and strange world, so very different from that which we had left behind. We were unaware of just how different it would become.

As the convoy journeyed northwards, I struggled to stay awake, determined to observe every possible detail. At times, I thought the countryside to be reminiscent of France. To the uninitiated eye, Israel displayed features of a modern country with motorways, cities and commercial centres. It was, however, punctuated by small rural dwellings, some almost primitive. Stopping midway on our journey towards the border with Lebanon, we availed of a sandwich and a welcome opportunity to stretch our legs. We would not have another break before our arrival at the border.

Journey's end for the drivers from the French logistic contingent brought us just across the international border into Lebanon, a land ravaged by war and hopelessly in need of redevelopment — but by whom? A large, makeshift carpark, used as an assembly point for Israeli armour, tanks and vehicles during their 1982 invasion of Lebanon, marked the changeover point to UN vehicles. The area contrasted sharply with the systematically irrigated, carefully reclaimed and cultivated kibbutz-style plantations of northern Israel. The change-over completed, we began our journey to the Irish battalion's area, but not before a short halt at the old custom post at Naquora a mile up the road. This sprawling complex of air-conditioned prefabs was now the location of Lebanon's UN headquarters and where those selected for appointments at HQ disembarked.

Venturing further north out of Lebanon's Israeli-controlled area to where the Fijian battalion was stationed, we met smart, impeccably dressed Pacific island men who greeted us in English by shouting "On the big Irish ball" — their version of "You lads are on the ball!" Simultaneously, they outlined the shape of a large imaginary ball with their fingers while broad smiles animated their faces. Travelling through the coastal

plain flanked by the Mediterranean Sea, the effects of war
were evident everywhere: bullet-riddled houses, some only
burnt-out shells, cratered roads, a damaged and neglected
infrastructure, everywhere the countryside's potential
unfulfilled. Running alongside the road were the rusting
remains of the railway built by Australian engineers in 1942
as an ammunition supply line after the Allied invasion of
Lebanon. Contrasting as it did with the countryside some
miles behind us in northern Israel, a more dramatic change
was immediately evident when we turned inland, leaving the
coastal road and climbing up steep gradients on narrow, pot-
holed roads as we headed for "the hills" and the Irish battalion
area.

Entering the area which was the responsibility of the
battalion from the foothills of the Himalayas, we received
friendly greetings of "Ram ram" (God be praised and God
preserve), salutations from the diminutive but very soldier-
like Nepalese Ghurkhas. Though only a journey of twenty-six
miles, the going was disproportionately slow as the large
convoy meandered its way upwards in the now-fading dusk.

Our arrival in the Irish battalion area was the most
dramatic of all. Battalion headquarters was situated in Tibnin,
a town sprawled across the top of a hill and dominated by the
crumbling ruins of a Crusader castle. Silhouetted against the
setting sun, a lone piper on top of a bunker played "The
Wearing of the Green", as welcoming a welcome as any tired,
bewildered Irishman could wish for. At last at our company
area, we arrived exhausted but elated to be finally in "the Leb"
proper. I, however, felt totally disorientated, lost and
unfamiliar with my surroundings. We were greeted warmly by
our company commander, pleased to have his complement
completed. The arrival of our chalk signified the official
commencement of the six-month tour, although operational
control had passed a week before during the handover.

I was surprised by how good facilities were, including
colour televisions and videos, and by the availability of so
many items. Makeshift shops were run by locals who had

become expert in supplying the needs of the UN battalions. I was surprised too by the terrain, more hilly than I had expected and at a higher altitude. I could not help comparing it with an arid, undulating Connemara or a west Cork terrain, sometimes quite dramatically so, with dry-stone-wall terracing evident everywhere. The closeness of the villages to one another and the smallness of the company area were further surprises, but what astonished me most was my feeling of complete disorientation. I realised I was trying too hard to take it all in; I needed time for sleep. It had been a long day, the first of many yet to come. Our journey from Leeside to the Litani had brought us not only to a different world but also to a world of differences.

WINTERISATION

08 November 1984

The culture shock of the Arabic setting was immediate. The early November sunlight pierced my bed's mosquito-net, causing me to wake early as warm air filled the room. From my window, I saw large flocks of goats and sheep being led down from the cooler mountain slopes to the warm lowlands and coastal plains, the first sign of the impending winter. Such a sight — hundreds of animals, all obeying a couple of shepherds and their dogs — was truly marvellous, straight out of the Bible. I noticed that the sheepdogs had their ears cut off and later learned that this was done in the belief that it would prevent disease.

These large flocks, the bells around their necks chiming away as they trotted along, created a lonely, plaintive music as they moved through the area. All that now remained of the rich harvest of fruit were a few pomegranates, withering on the branches that were out of reach. The faded browns and fawns of the dead grasses cloaked the countryside and looked ominous as the dark winter clouds replaced the clear blue skies, making the land look cold and bleak. In the distance, prayers from the Koran calling the faithful to prayer echoed from the loudspeaker on a minaret of a mosque.

The operational situation in our area was dominated by three factors: the presence of LAUI militia gangs in Barachit village; the *de facto* pro-Israeli forces or Christian militia presence in Bayt Yahon; and the movement of Israeli defence force personnel through our company's area. Deployed in the south-east section of the battalion area of operations, and nearest the Christian enclave, we would be the first to encounter the pro-Israeli Christian militia and the Israeli army's movements entering the UN area of operations from the south. It was our job to monitor and control all traffic and to act as an early-warning system for vehicles approaching from the Israeli-controlled area. Three villages were located within our company area. In the largest of these, Barachit, was a local militia gang checkpoint, one of the two "hot spots" identified during the officer briefing as having the potential for confrontation.

Our company was committed to maintaining five checkpoints, four observation posts, a foot and mobile patrol programme with armoured personnel carriers, and one security guard at company headquarters. Total strength was just over a hundred, of which six were officers. In addition to their specific responsibilities, all officers except the company commander rotated the role of company duty officer. The company's second-in-command ran the company headquarters and took charge of logistical and administrative details.

In on-the-ground peacekeeping, the soldier's role as a catalyst for peace rather than as an instrument of war is the responsibility of the company's lieutenants — the platoon commanders — something completely different from home and more demanding. By definition, peacekeeping operations are established in areas of conflict where acts of violence and breaches of international and local agreements could be daily occurrences. Although it has been said that peacekeeping is not a suitable job for soldiers, it is only soldiers who can do the job.

Now, in early November, "winterisation" was the buzz word as we made our accommodation ready for the cloudbursts and torrential rain which proved to be quite unlike anything we had experienced in Ireland. Window refitments, installation of paraffin-fuelled Damascus oil heaters, and general water-proofing of billets were all undertaken, but not before we had gone through a thorough orientation. Having arrived with mixed emotions, apprehensive and excited at facing the unknown, we were bombarded with information during the first few days. Orders were read and explained; personal weapons, helmets, flak jackets and blue UN berets were issued. Drills were rehearsed, including fire drills and "groundhogs" (going to the bunkers in the event of shelling), along with the scheme of defence — taking up exact positions around the post's perimeter during an actual or threatened attack.

The company's three platoons had specific responsibilities. Two platoons were deployed outside the company head-quarters. The third platoon, mine, secured the company headquarters, operating a security checkpoint outside HQ. As the "in platoon", those deployed inside company HQ, we also acted as a company reserve should incidents arise in the outlying platoon positions.

21 November 1984

After adjusting to the strangeness of our new surroundings, names and places both on maps and on the ground were becoming more familiar to us. The early winter, while not especially wet, witnessed many heavy rainstorms which filled the irrigation tanks that were placed below the roads, acting as excellent breeding grounds for the mosquito. Cold winds blew down from the snow-capped Mount Hermon. On top of this much-fought-over mountain range, some 7,500 feet above sea level, was an Israeli listening post which was of immense strategic and tactical importance to their military machine. Under its antenna, a sophisticated array of electronic intelligence-gathering and signal equipment was concreted into the bedrock of the mountain.

In many ways, arriving in South Lebanon was like a return to our own feudal past. The people lived in a simple, rural, under-organised society, one with a high moral code. With the family as the binding core, the village was their world and its elders their authority. They were a society let down by the Beirut government whose efforts were not directed towards its people. Party and personal politics took precedence over the people, and most of the wealth of the ruling families was kept outside the country. It didn't filter down, so the base of the society couldn't broaden.

This unstable political and financial system further upset an unstable society with its large Christian population in a Muslim area. Civil war had ravaged the country and carved up the whole of Lebanon into fiefdoms with an ever-shifting series of alliances causing complication and confusion. Foreign involvement made local issues even more difficult with Lebanon's geographical position at a crossroads between the European West and the Arab Middle East. Since the land itself was unable to provide sufficient subsistence, the Lebanese economy was substantially supported by wealthy returned emigrants and by remittances from those who remained abroad. We could not help but respect these people, surviving as they did in an environment made hostile by climate, land, invasion, colonisation and war.

The winter sound I remember most was the plaintive cry of the lapwing, the green plover, as it flew over this upland winter wasteland in search of food. This bird came to symbolise the determination of a hardy people who eked out a simple living during the winter months.

* * *

The role of company duty officer was becoming more familiar. It involved reporting to the company commander in maintaining a watching brief over the entire company area twenty-four hours a day. Located in the company communications centre or radio room, it was my job to maintain the daily log book and inform the company commander of any incidents such as shootings or the possibility of confrontation. The duty officer also had to conduct a minimum of two patrols of the company area both by day and by night. Retiring to bed after midnight, duty officers were the first to be woken if required by the signal operator. Finally, we briefed the company commander early the next morning before he went to the "morning brief" in battalion headquarters. On his return, the commander disseminated any essential information to his own conference.

Ironically, being the "in platoon" became almost as regimented as it was in our home barracks in Ireland. Except for the obvious Middle Eastern situation and the South Lebanon setting, the Irish battalion's peacekeeping routine had become largely uneventful. Resistance activities were concentrated further north of us, so it fell to other UN battalions to confront the worst elements of the Israeli army's "Iron Fist" policy against the villages deemed sympathetic to the Sh'ite Muslim guerrillas. Since the 1982 Israeli invasion, UN policy permitted Israeli troops and Shin Bet intelligence operatives to pass unhindered through its checkpoints. This, and the continuing pro-Israeli local militia and Israeli army presence within the Irish battalion area, meant that the nature of the operational situation was always unpredictable. The surface appearance of calm and routine belied the ever-present threat of violence.

During periods of relative stability, peacekeepers can become victims of their own success. The routine performance of its platoons and the conduct of its members often attract criticisms which might otherwise go unmentioned, even unnoticed, during more active periods or tense situations. This was particularly true of the company headquarters' "in platoon". Persistent comment, especially early in a tour, could undermine the confidence of platoon commanders who are already struggling to find their bearings in relation to the terrain, the culture and the situation, but especially in the command of their platoon. This was particularly true when dealing with platoon members who had already seen overseas service. Although this was very much dependent on the individual platoon commander's character, personality and leadership style, he may already be attempting to strike a balance between acting upon every observation, criticism or comment, and allowing these to have an adverse effect upon the mood and morale of his platoon.

Invariably, the platoon sergeant would have seen overseas duty, as indeed would most of the platoon's corporals. Here, teamwork and loyalty win through — if the commander has the common sense to listen to these men and trust in their experience. Sometimes, a platoon commander can be just plain unlucky to have a run of unrelated incidents occurring one after the other and involving individuals of his platoon, leading to much unneeded and undeserved notice.

My platoon sergeant, known to all as "Sergeant Paddy", a sturdy and affable North Tipperary man, was five years my senior with four previous tours in Lebanon. He and I identified the possible difficulties and were determined to maintain the platoon's effectiveness. We resolved to emphasise the positive and created a programme of projects to be completed in advance of inspection by the battalion commander. So began a period of intense and fruitful "housekeeping" of the company headquarters and the reconstruction of the platoon's checkpoint blockhouses, along with much painting and whitewashing.

As an old army saying goes: "If it moves, salute it. If it doesn't, whitewash it." Just before dusk one day, I noticed that a local's donkey had remained stationary for too long... I prayed for rain that night!

STRANGE SOLDIERING

26 November 1984

The relative ease with which the battalion had settled in belied the realities of a volatile situation. We soon became accustomed to the pace of events, and while matters were categorised as calm, they were not without incident. We were constantly finding and disposing of cluster bombs or dealing with minor situations when the local militia attempted to carry weapons through our checkpoints or to pass in their uniforms. In addition, monitoring Israeli troop movements highlighted that the circumstances could change rapidly from peace to conflict. This very unpredictability gave rise to a low but nonetheless palpable level of tension. There was also a soldier's unease that, as peacekeepers, we were not deployed in the usual military mode. All duties — manning checkpoints and observation posts, patrolling and reporting — had to be performed impartially, in all circumstances and in all weathers, with a consistent interpretation of standard operating procedures.

The Irish area had always been one of the UN's most active. The Israeli reinvasion of Lebanon brought about a number of changes: the expulsion of Palestinian guerrilla fighters; an Israeli army presence; and the creation of surrogate pro-Israeli militias in the UN areas. The UN in general, and the Irish battalion in particular, had to adjust its policy in response to this situation. The speed of adjustment became a vital part in overall planning. No matter how things evolved, our posts had to be secure, our checkpoints strong, and everything capable of being reinforced quickly in order to achieve and maintain control. And if there had to be a compromise in our natural role as soldiers, there was to be none on personal safety.

* * *

With a twenty-four-hour work routine, a programme of entertainment, sports and social events was needed. At home, a night out would be taken for granted. Here, with such limited resources, we became extraordinarily adept and cast ourselves into unthought-of roles: bingo hosts, dart competition organisers, travel advisers, even choir-masters. Participation was encouraged, and the young officers particularly were heavily involved. In my case, this included road-running, uncharted territory for a ball player... and "fun while you run" it wasn't. The company had a good team and I was counted on to be "placed", so in good army style, I gave it all I had, participating in any event the hills of South Lebanon threw my way.

Most daunting by far was preparing the platoon to participate in the inter-platoon talent competition. This undertaking was particularly intimidating because I saw no obvious signs of talent. My mistake, for in our midst we had singers, musicians, amateur actors — performers aplenty — and both I and "Sergeant Paddy" became overnight chore-ographers.

27 November 1984
One act performed on the night of the show, and one which I had not seen rehearsed, was a sketch which I slowly realised was a caricature of the company commander and myself. Humorous but tactful, its detailed demonstration of our mannerisms was uncannily accurate.

15 December 1984
The best-organised of platoon business, no matter how urgent, was often interrupted by visitors. I frequently had to brief the many staff officers from Lebanon's UN headquarters, the

passing officers from Observer Group Lebanon and members of the media both from Ireland and elsewhere. Although these arrivals often occurred with minimum notice, they were always welcomed and provided a break from the busy routine. Briefings took place on the roof of the converted house which formed the focal point of the company headquarters. The usual format consisted of ground orientation, company deployment, recent incidents, and a question-and-answer session, followed by an informal discussion over a cup of tea.

It now seemed ages since we had left Ireland and I had long since ceased to think in terms of things Irish. However, a surprising opportunity arose to spend Christmas in the place where it all began, the Holy Land. Applications for limited places on the battalion tour were sought and I became an eager pilgrim. Brought up in the solid Catholic tradition, this would be an opportunity to visit and experience the legendary locations.

22 December 1984

With a copy of the Holy Land tour itinerary in my bag, I woke extra early on the morning of departure and joined the convoy at battalion headquarters bound for Naquora. As we journeyed southwards, I noticed much birdlife. The Mediterranean's warming effect on the coastal plain meant that the lowlands were richer in vegetation and insects, resulting in large numbers of resident species.

On arrival in Naquora, we changed from uniform to civilian gear in preparation for crossing the border into Israel and our trip to Jerusalem via Tiberias. It wasn't a simple change of clothes in the ordinary sense — more a transformation, or a re-transformation and a totally unexpected novelty. After seven weeks in uniform, we could no longer envision ourselves in anything else. Then there it was: the sudden realisation that since arriving in Lebanon, everything we did was single-mindedly concentrated on the platoon. Now, we could be ourselves. The change of attire was both symbolic and elating... I was enjoying this Holy Land tour already.

In Israel, diversity is the rule rather than the exception. Over half of the population is native-born, most first and second generation. The people are predominantly Jews, with a large number of Arab citizens making up the largest portion of the country's non-Jewish minority. The co-existence of Jew and Arab had not been without tension, conflict and the periodic flare-up, beginning when the state of Israel was established in 1948. Control of Jerusalem's Old City is at the heart of this conflict, symbolic of the fanaticism and bloodshed that have divided Jews and Muslims for centuries. To Jews, the Temple Mount represents the foundation stone of their history, where King Solomon built a temple containing the Ark of the Covenant. Destroyed by the Babylonians, rebuilt by King Herod, destroyed again by Romans in 70 AD, nothing remains except the Wailing Wall, now a revered holy place for Jews. This same site, covering some 35 acres, is known to the Muslims as the Noble Sanctuary from whence the Prophet Mohammed made a night journey to heaven after instructing his followers to face Jerusalem when they prayed. In the seventh century, the Muslims built a mosque with a vast golden cupola on this site known as the Dome of the Rock. Nearby is the Al-Aqsa Mosque. The entire site, a holy place for Jews and Muslims alike, represents the region's wrath of ages.

Service in Israel's armed forces is mandatory. All eligible men and women are drafted at age eighteen, men for three years and women for two, with men liable for reserve duty until age fifty-five and women to age twenty-four. During our tour in Lebanon, the Israeli Defence Force was composed of a small standing army, a cadre of career officers and non-commissioned officers, as well as men and women draftees and reserve officers. The reserve forces which made up the bulk of the army's manpower were regularly called up for training and service. Thus, the Israeli Defence Force is a citizens' army, with those in and out of uniform virtually interchangeable. Armed Israeli soldiers were evident everywhere, whether on duty or waiting in groups for public transport. Their presence ensured that weapons and uniforms continued to prevail upon one's consciousness.

After the desolate rock and scrub-covered hillsides of South Lebanon, Jerusalem offered not only holy sites but a modern city with the chance of rest and relaxation. The hot shower after our five-hour journey could be enjoyed at length... no concerns about wasting water, an ever-present consideration in the hills of South Lebanon. I found Jerusalem to be a city of contrasts. In spite of an impressive Old City, it was otherwise new and planned. There were Arabs, Jews, Christians, Armenians in a place of mutual reverence which was now hugely commercialised.

23 December 1984

A walking tour of the atmospheric Old City was on the itinerary after we oriented ourselves on the Mount of Olives with a panoramic view of the principal landmarks. The strong Biblical sense was evident, but only if you were able to detach yourself from the chaotic calls of the trading stallholders along the alleyways. Leather goods, brass and all manner of souvenirs were available in abundance on the Via Dolorosa, held to be Jesus' route as he carried his cross to Calvary. Historic and symbolic, Jerusalem is a holy city for three major religions — Judaism, Christianity and Islam — and has been much fought over both in ancient and recent times. Our tour allowed us to savour its special atmosphere both by day and night, and for me, the highlight would be the celebration of midnight mass on Christmas eve in the Church of the Nativity, St Catherine's in Bethlehem.

24 December 1984

After standing in a packed Latin mass for $2^1/_2$ hours, and having endured lengthy and elaborate security measures, I was feeling somewhat disappointed. This, however, did not diminish my appreciation of the sense of occasion. I felt very drawn to, and conscious of, the values which had been nurtured in me during my Irish upbringing.

Earlier that day, we had travelled south through the Negev Desert and experienced life along the Dead Sea, the lowest point on earth, with its therapeutic waters, black mud and mineral springs found nowhere else in the world. At Ein Gedi, a desert oasis, we bathed in the sea itself. Containing 21% salt, bathers are so buoyant that they can read a book or a newspaper while floating on the surface.

25 December 1984

Christmas Day in Jerusalem was an ordinary working day, devoid of seasonal atmosphere. A free day on our tour, we ventured south to the fortress rock of Masada. The site has now been excavated and reconstructed to tell the story of 980 zealot Jews who escaped the Roman sacking of Jerusalem in 70 AD by taking refuge in Herod the Great's elaborate winter palace on the mountain of Masada. For three years, 10,000 Roman soldiers camped at the base of the mountain, laying siege to the Jewish rebels. The tragic outcome of this epic would be unbelievable if it were not true. The Jews took on the might of Rome and claimed their own victory, choosing death rather than slavery and submission. In the course of time, Masada has become a traditional place of pilgrimage on Hanukah, the Jewish feast of light and heroism.

Since the establishment of the state of Israel, the new recruits of its armour corps have been sworn in at Masada, using the symbolism of "Masada shall not fall again" to forge an awareness of its history among the younger generations of Israel.

* * *

Our Holy Land tour now over, an early morning bus journey from Jerusalem to Naquora left me time to ponder my visit. It had indeed been a holy place, but I also had the sinking feeling that it was a holy mess with ancient enmities which could render it a holy hell. In spite of the joint disappointments of over-commercialism and thinly veiled conflict, my personal pilgrimage had been worthwhile. I felt rejuvenated. The time, distance and change of atmosphere allowed me a renewed perspective on South Lebanon. I was going to need it.

ESTIMATE OF THE SITUATION

08 January 1985

The first inter-platoon rotations took place without incident. Having largely maintained the shape of the platoon intact, we exited company headquarters and took up positions in a village less than a mile outside our former location. Platoon headquarters was in a house across from the mosque in the village square, its narrow, winding, cobbled streets flanked by irregular, tightly packed, flat-roofed houses, making it very Biblical in character. When the Israeli army invasion began in 1978, the entire population left the village, turning it into a ghost town. When the UN forces arrived and the Irish battalion took over the house in the village square, many of the villagers returned.

A feature of life during this time was the constant shelling of the village by the pro-Israeli Christian militia under Major Haddad who were trying to flush out Palestinian guerrillas. Because of this shelling, Lebanese sympathy for the Palestinians began to wane and many drifted away from the area. Amal was now gaining in popularity although it did not take part in any military activities. After the Israeli army's reinvasion of Lebanon in June 1982, UN influence in the area was curtailed somewhat and the Christian militia tried to exercise more control in the village. A local militia was set up and supplied with weapons, uniforms and equipment by the Israeli army. Their leader, Hassein Abdul Nabbi, was an unstable individual. Irrational and unreliable, he was easily excited. A dangerous man, he was described by some as a psychopath and was associated with several murders in the village. He could call on twenty to thirty men who would take up weapons at short notice and also had people in the village who would pass information to him. He used classic hoodlum tactics to intimidate and control the area. Controlled and financed by the Israeli army, he and his gang set up an illegal checkpoint in the village. Although Irish battalion soldiers tried to negotiate the withdrawal of Nabbi and his gang, UN operations decided to put a blocking or containing checkpoint on each side of the illegal position. It was the Irish battalion's task to prevent Nabbi's pro-Israeli gang from leaving their position while armed or in uniform and entering the village proper to exercise any type of control. The gang reacted by abusing Irish soldiers, provoking them and otherwise hindering them in doing their job. This led to confrontations, the deployment of reserves and tension-filled stand-offs which were usually diffused through negotiation.

These stressful confrontations sometimes led to Irish battalion soldiers being fired on and otherwise harassed. This had serious implications for platoon members on continuous duty, especially the new arrivals... us. Accordingly, I undertook an estimate of the situation we found ourselves in, reflecting on how best to approach any likely problems.

It was immediately apparent that platoon morale was much improved as a result of rotating into the village. It was ironic that we should welcome the move to this notorious hot spot, but the platoon could now be identified with its own particular area of responsibility and specific tasks. We had a mission and the means to achieve it: the essential ingredients for contentment in the military mind.

11 January 1985

Minor confrontations, shootings and other incidents were occurring in other company areas of the Irish battalion area and throughout the UN zone in general. It was, however, a further irony that a significant shooting incident took place on the day after our rotation into the village. It happened in an Irish battalion location which was not considered particularly hostile, thus underlining the volatile and unpredictable circumstances within which we operated. Unprovoked, militiamen had fired at and narrowly missed the neighbouring Irish company's duty officer as he approached them on a checkpoint. The Irish sentries on the checkpoint post justifiably judged the situation to be life-threatening and returned fire. One pro-Israeli militiaman was seriously injured.

The battalion commander immediately ordered that all inter-post movements were to have a minimum of two vehicles, with no less than two armed persons in each. All persons were to be armed in any movement outside their posts. Exercising was to be in groups, with a mobile escort, and any drinking was restricted to a maximum of two cans of beer. Mindful of the area's tradition of "an eye for an eye and a tooth for a tooth", such precautions were imperative. If a local militiaman or paramilitary was killed by a UN soldier, even when acting under extreme provocation and in self-defence, local tradition required the victim's family and friends to take the life of a UN peacekeeper in return. They would choose the time and the place; in these circumstances, everyone was vulnerable. There was also a local tradition of *sulha* or blood reconciliation in which, for a compensatory exchange, usually a monetary one, the blood feud and obligation for revenge could be satisfied without further loss of life.

Our checkpoints were strengthened, and platoon commanders were dispatched to their platoon locations where they were to stay until further notice. Armoured cars patrolled constantly between posts. The entire battalion was confined to their posts that night.

In spite of this, we were glad of the chance to settle in to our new surroundings. We hardly knew ourselves. The platoon headquarters itself was fortified with sandbags, barbed wire and galvanised sheeting. The observation post and machine gun position on the roof were manned constantly. The radio and land-line field phones were also on the roof.

Our current predicament reminded me of a major event which took place in the early years of the UN's mission in Lebanon when there was an attempted takeover of the village of At-Tiri in the Irish battalion area. At-Tiri was strategically important to the UN as it lay in the so-called "Christian enclave" which was controlled by the Major Haddad's paramilitary forces. It also provided access to Hill 880 from which the villages of Haddatha, Harris and Tibnin could be dominated. The village was therefore vital to UNIFIL and to the Irish battalion in particular.

The week-long confrontation saw both sides introduce reinforcements. The Christian militia gradually increased the tension by opening fire on Irish battalion armoured personnel carriers. They escalated the confrontation further by increasing the intensity of their firing and by using heavy-calibre machine guns and tank rounds. Fire was returned, which stopped them from advancing on the Irish positions. Small arms fire continued each day and UN peacekeepers returned fire when fired on. Sadly, two UN lives were lost: Private Stephen Griffin from the Irish battalion, and Private Soronaivalu, a Fijian member of the UNIFIL Reserve pressed into action during the confrontation. There was also a Christian militia casualty.

Later, three Irish battalion peacekeepers were abducted by the Christian militia. Two were shot dead in revenge for the militiaman who had died at At-Tiri: Privates Derek Smallhorne and Thomas Barrett. The third, Private John O'Mahony, though seriously injured having been shot in cold blood at close range, managed to escape. I remembered receiving news of these sinister events and the cruel murders during the pre-commissioning dinner for my cadet class two weeks before becoming an officer. It left me with a marked and grim impression of the realities of peacekeeping in South Lebanon. Now, four years later, these realities were again a possibility. I resolved to do everything I could to ensure the safety and protection of the platoon.

12 January 1985
The previous day's shooting had created a state of high alert in the battalion. It was also the cause of increased activity among

the local militiamen, and there was much to-ing and fro-ing from their checkpoint in the village. The tension was mounting; we were constantly being told to be conscious of our own security. We were already alert to the possibility of our checkpoint sentries being snatched or fired on from passing cars, or of one of our patrols being ambushed.

It was time for me and Sergeant Paddy to increase our presence at the checkpoints, on the roof of the platoon head-quarters and on patrols. It was time, too, to express our confidence in the men and to reinforce their confidence in themselves. It was critical to reassure the platoon of the sequence of reactions which might be required in given situations, to strike the balance between restraint and that split-second judgment to open fire. Getting it wrong in either eventuality could prove fatal.

Keeping the peace implies protecting the innocent and improving the quality of life for those who live where the peace is being kept. However, there was little doubting the deterioration of the operational situation. Having erupted, the violence so close to the surface was likely to manifest itself sooner rather than later in this village hot-bed. But how? And when? I wondered how I might react, both as an individual and as a platoon commander. It was a fascination tempered with dread at the possibility of reacting inadequately, or of being afraid. The dread was a fear of fear itself, or more precisely, a fear of showing fear, a fear of failure, of losing control, of not being able to cope with the speed of reactions required. I was at a loss. I did not know what state or presence of mind was required to master the real situation. I always came full circle, back to being fascinated by what would be required of me in such a situation. I sensed I was not alone in thinking these thoughts: each man of the platoon was already at war... with himself. Then came the news that an Irish battalion vehicle in a neighbouring Irish battalion company area had been fired on: no casualties reported. It had to be only a matter of time before we came under fire ourselves. In the event, it was almost immediate.

14 January 1985

A local man reported that a villager had been abducted by the
local militia gang and taken to their checkpoint. Immediately,
a purpose-built "stop gap" which further impeded movement
and blocked the roadway was put into effect. Sentries at Irish
battalion checkpoints also positioned tank stops. Armoured
personnel carriers blocked the roads. Checkpoints were
reinforced. Movement in the company area was effectively
frozen. The company reserve was dispatched to our location
to assist us in our efforts to frustrate any attempted abduction.

Now aware that we were reacting to the alleged abduction,
the local militiamen were displeased to be discovered so early
and to see that we were taking steps to address the situation.
Our reaction had been timely and complete. Without
escalating matters, it was both the minimum and the
maximum that could be attempted. What mattered now was
the militiamen's response.

Suddenly, the staccato of short bursts of small arms fire
shook the stillness. My wondering was over. Having come
under fire, my immediate response was a momentary freeze-
frame. It could only be likened to virtual reality in reverse.
The real seemed unreal and gave way to concerns of any
resulting casualties. Radios started, with reports of the gunfire
being called into company headquarters. On the field-phone
land-line, the company commander wanted an immediate
report of the situation. Everything was happening at once.

So there it was, our baptism of fire. Strangely enough, my
overriding sense was one of relief. While undoubtedly
stressful, it was not specifically frightening. But I was
concerned about what would happen next. There was no
script, no pre-planned scenario, no pre-arranged roles, no
responsible authority overseeing a logical, controlled
conclusion. Yet we had to manage it somehow, and manage it
now.

Curiously, while all these thoughts were going through my
mind at lightening speed and there were many competing
demands for my attention, being fired upon meant I had

reached an unspoken military milestone, a coming of age, so
to speak.

An initiation had taken place, but now what? Uncertainty
again, and a dangerous uncertainty at that. As soldiers, our
training taught us that, once fired upon, we should locate the
enemy, give an accurate fire order and bring controlled,
effective fire to bear. But as peacekeepers, we were eye-to-eye
with the aggressor and had to respond with disciplined
restraint by absorbing the aggression.

What next? Check the platoon. See that they had taken up
proper protection. Then continue to sit it out, allow the
situation to settle and attempt to negotiate. Now to respond to
the   company   commander,   Commandant   Padraigh
O'Callaghan, a tough, uncompromising but fair-minded
officer from County Roscommon whose game plan for when
things got tight was well worked out.

At least the moment of uncertainty had not given way to
confusion, and confusion to fear, and fear to a failure to
analyse the situation properly. Shortly, three car-loads of
Israeli army personnel arrived in the village to calm the gang.
The Israelis were now directly accountable for the fate of the
abducted villager. On this occasion, because we were prepared
to go the distance and call their bluff, he was released.

FACE TO FACE

21 January 1985

The Lebanese winter twilight is not one that lingers. A veil of darkness is drawn on the mid-afternoon dusk within minutes. It had been a tense week since the abduction incident, a week in which the company's platoon commanders were offered the facility of arming themselves with a rifle. Each one availed of the offer.

News of the wounded militiaman's deteriorating condition, although it eventually stabilised, had heightened the situation. During this week, too, the Israeli government announced a plan for the unilateral redeployment of Israeli forces in three phases; a few days later it was formally presented to the Naquora conference. This conference had come about after the UN Secretary General had approached the governments of Israel and Lebanon, suggesting that they begin negotiations as soon as possible on the withdrawal of Israeli forces from Lebanese territory and related security arrangements in Southern Lebanon. After consultations with these governments, the Secretary General convened a conference of military representatives of the two countries at Lebanon's UN headquarters in Naquora. The conference met intermittently for months. From the outset, the Lebanese representatives insisted on the full withdrawal of Israeli forces from Lebanese territory and the subsequent deployment of the Lebanese army, together with the UN force, down to the international boundary in accordance with UN Security Council Resolution 425 (1978).

The Israeli representative, however, took the position that while Israel would accept a limited UN presence in the south,

Israeli-backed local forces should be responsible for security arrangements in the southernmost part of Lebanon.

The war in Lebanon had become increasingly unpopular in Israel itself. The Israeli government was finding it harder and harder to justify it, especially among the younger people. It was costing them huge amounts of money daily, necessitating a heavy war tax on items and incomes, and adding considerably to Israel's already high inflation rate and cost of living. The war was particularly costly in manpower, which was also increasingly unacceptable.

News of the Israeli army's impending withdrawal from Lebanon had operational implications for our future situation in the south. The lingering unease was exacerbated by the increased paranoia of the Israeli-backed militia gangs who feared revenge attacks with the departure of their patrons.

That evening shortly after twilight, the village was cast into darkness. As an eerie silence fell, we received a message from our company headquarters that two local men had been abducted and brought to the militia gang checkpoint in the village. Contacting our two containing checkpoints, I received no confirmation of any likely movement; there had been little activity to and from the checkpoint all afternoon and evening.

We were ordered to send out a foot patrol to conduct a limited reconnaissance and investigate further. I went to the roof of the platoon headquarters with an armed supporting group to maintain line-of-sight as far as possible. The patrol hadn't progressed very far when a hail of fire from within the village ricocheted off the roadway, creating bright red and yellow sparks. The noise of the gunfire reverberated deafeningly around the village square. It was sudden; it was dramatic; it was raw; it was violent. And if fear is tension realised, it was fearful. If my immediate reaction to gunfire a week before had been relief mixed with concern, it was now definitely fear: fear for the safety of the patrol. My body went suddenly cold. My heart pounded and I was involuntarily taking breaths in short gasps. My eyes never strayed from the patrol's position. I seemed to be able to take in a wide field of vision. Meanwhile, in the distance, I could hear the roar of the engines of our armoured cars: the company reserve was on its way.

Within seconds, Sergeant Paddy doused the platoon headquarters' lights and ordered the remainder of the HQ personnel to the roof, all armed, helmeted and with flak jackets. Our position was being reinforced from both sides of the village to support the deployment of the patrol. Then we waited… and waited.

I had to fight the soldier's natural reaction to order covering fire which would allow our patrol to withdraw in good order. I could read that thought going through the minds of everyone on the flat rooftop, but restraint was called for. This restraint was contrary to the urge to counter fear by reacting; instead, the fear had to be endured.

After what seemed an age, and without further gunfire, the patrol withdrew and made their way back to our location. Shortly after, our armoured personnel carriers arrived in the village square, their lights slicing the darkness. We stood-to for a further hour and a half, during which time no further incidents occurred. With no discernible movements, we stood down.

To satisfy the inevitable demands for details at the following morning's conference, I had to write the report while events and timings were fresh in my mind. The report complete, I remained awake and made reassuring visits to the sentries on the roof and at our checkpoints.

Between visits, and already in a writing mode, I caught up on my personal letters. From early in the tour, I had appreciated the importance of receiving letters from family and friends, transporting me thousands of miles back home to Ireland. Post was a vital link, a crucial contact, a paper touchstone, with some letters being read and re-read by home-sick soldiers starved of contact with their loved ones. Close attention was always paid to the receipt of mail. The lack of it was often an early indication of problems arising home-side and sometimes necessitated a phone-patch to Ireland. This required a conscious effort from platoon commanders and sergeants, as did the constant watchful eye for any adverse reaction to the receipt of bad news. But this was all part of the constant man-management which was never regarded as a chore and soon became second nature.

My report and letter-writing finished, I reflected on the recent happenings. The progressively deteriorating operational situation was characterised by the increasingly violent nature of confrontations. The excitement of recent days had reinforced the fact that these were not blank rounds of ammunition being directed our way and underlined the possibility that someone might become a casualty. This anxiety had to be addressed. Having come face to face with fear, I was now ready to come face to face with the fearful: the psychopathic leader of the local militia henchmen, a notoriously dangerous and unpredictable killer who had to be dealt with using extreme caution.

22 January 1985

The platoon's experience of live incidents had been a maturing process, a growing up. In a sense, coming face to face with these realities had caused us to suffer a loss of innocence. But it also imbued us with a strong feeling of self-confidence and personal credibility. This helped our platoon to gel, to achieve a strong cohesion and integrity. For my part, my own belief in myself as a platoon commander had been assured. I had also come face to face with myself... and my curiosity had been satisfied.

Experience had taught us that we should arrange to meet Nabbi, the local militia gang leader, at or near our own checkpoint — and not his — where he might attempt to take those with whom he was negotiating hostage. Young, only a few years older than myself, slightly built with curly hair and beard to match, I was disappointed by his lack of presence but wouldn't allow myself to be disarmed by it. In any event, I was largely present only to observe and listen. It was my company commander who would do the talking and enquire about the reported kidnapping of the villagers. This gave me the time and space to be one pace removed from the hustings and to observe the countenance of a killer. Could I discern any tell-tale feature, facial detail or mannerism which would distinguish him as predisposed to extremes of violence? None presented itself.

My musings were interrupted almost immediately. Hardly had the discussions commenced when Nabbi suddenly started shouting and gesticulating wildly, objecting to those points which had only just been made. He turned on his heel and strode off. My first meeting, and it was over as soon at it began. My company commander left the village and returned to his company headquarters while I withdrew to the deserted village square.

Any consideration of these events was short-lived as the roof-top sentry began waving frantically to attract my attention. Entering the platoon headquarters, I went straight to the roof and could scarcely believe my eyes — the militia gang was deploying in strength. Heavy machine guns, mortars, riflemen were all being positioned, made ready for a fire fight. Tempted to similarly deploy, I sought and took my platoon sergeant's council and had the platoon stand-to, but internally within the house and out of the line-of-sight of the militia. I contacted our checkpoint sentries and told them not to be seen to react. They were to appear nonchalant, but within easy reach of cover.

Our apparent non-reaction must have perplexed Nabbi as he once again approached our checkpoint. Approaching from my side, I saw Nabbi and four menacing henchmen, haphazardly cradling their Kalashnikov rifles in their arms. Behind them, in the middle distance, stood his gang, intent on wrong-doing. Walking towards them, I was struck by how outrageously unreal it all seemed, resembling a scene from a western movie with the town's sheriff meeting the bandits… only in a Biblical setting. But it was all too real. This *was* happening, and we *were* involved. This was neither the Wild West nor the Old Testament. This was South Lebanon, where life could be dangerous, and short.

Nervous, I was nonetheless in earnest and quietly determined to press my point home. During the customary handshakes, I engaged each man in eye-to-eye contact with a firm grip and firm stare, not challenging but not meek either. It was then that I noticed that one of his henchmen was cross-eyed which somehow seemed ludicrously comical. But in this highly charged situation, he also exuded a coldness that was both stark and savage. Pointedly, I glanced behind me to reassure myself that my checkpoint party was taking it all in, poised to react if required. It wasn't necessary, but neither was my gesture lost on the militiamen.

Initially, nothing was said by either Nabbi or me and I allowed the silence to continue. I kept him fixed with my eyes, non-verbally communicating that I was not about to be intimidated. We had been fired on twice and that was enough: next time we were returning fire. Once our conversation began, I was careful to ensure that there was nothing offensive or high-handed in my tone or manner. I could not be seen to be talking down to him in front of his own men.

Nabbi had brought an unwilling villager to interpret. I made my point, and he his, that he was fearful of being attacked by the Amal or Hezbullah. No more was said: there was no more to say. I would have to enquire about the reported kidnapping when deployed weapons had ceased to be part of the scene. I could develop a relationship later. For now, an understanding was required. I stared hard into his eyes, hoping to detect a split-second indication of what his next unpredictable move might be. In the event, I was surprised yet again with a broad smile, a bear hug and a handshake… that would do nicely. Now to see if this meant he would de-escalate the situation by calling his gang to order. It did.

Relieved, I walked back through the Irish checkpoint were a sentry, Private Philip O'Regan, commented: "Jesus, Sir, I think Nabbi's in love with you!"

He wasn't, and somehow, I knew there would be another day.

SALAAM... SHALOM

The remainder of the platoon's time in the village had been one of incidents, threats, stand-offs and close firings. The lingering tension was both physically and psychologically taxing. I felt tired and mentally drained. There were also frustrations on the home front. By now, some media observers were beginning to ask whether the UN Irish in Lebanon were facing greater risks than could possibly be justified by what they could hope to achieve there.

It was with some relief that, on balance, it was appreciated that peacekeeping in Lebanon was a painstaking business which required patience and skills of a very special nature. We were proud of the UN's and the Irish battalion's achievements. But for the force's presence, an almost tenfold increase in the population of South Lebanon, controlled by the UN, could never have been achieved. We provided some stability to the area, a degree of normalisation which, despite the deteriorating situation, could be used as a platform for future progress and development. This could not be surrendered lightly. In short, our presence was valid, with our efforts and sacrifices worthwhile.

For all that, successful peacekeeping demanded a huge effort within which we had also to concentrate on the day-to-day routine and the mundane housekeeping tasks. There were constant checks to ensure we had sufficient supplies of water, stocks of food and gas to cook it with. There were hygiene and sanitation considerations, particularly the arrival of what became known as the "honey wagon", a local contractor who emptied the post's septic tanks. Rabies was endemic in the region, and while a shotgun was available if required, it was not always wise to use it during times of tension. Sandbags dropped from a height were sufficient to scare away any doubtful creatures. Other health requirements necessitated the careful maintenance of a register, a daily record of the issue and use of malaria tablets. The supply of diesel for generators had to be considered, and while this was all very much in a day's work, none of it could be taken for granted.

Leave was therefore a welcome change of scene, speed and style. I had organised to take leave to Egypt with a cadet school classmate, Michael McGinley from Donegal. He was in the second of the infamous Irish battalion hot spots, and life had been no less hectic for him either.

20 February 1985

For all its size, noise, frenzied and bustling bazaars, crazy drivers, tumultuous traffic and millions of people, Cairo had a welcome peace about it. "Salaam" is the Arabic word for "peace", and I was at peace because I was no longer a platoon commander in the Land of the Cedar but a tourist in the Land of the Pharaohs.

Located where the Nile valley widens into the flat, fertile delta, Cairo has been at the centre of Egyptian life for millennia. The largest city in Africa and one of the most densely populated places on earth, ancient Cairo's legacy included the Giza pyramids, one of the seven wonders of the world, sphinxes, mummies and hieroglyphics. The Khan el Khalili *souk* is a teeming handcrafts bazaar with a mesmerising labyrinth of crowded streets and alleyways, known for its golden, silver and bronze crafted products, hand-made tapestries and carpets, leather goods and perfumes.

The pace of Cairo was chaotic and we had to throw ourselves into its crazed rhythm to appreciate its uniqueness, its extraordinary blend of old and new, ancient and modern, its grand palaces and mosques. So numerous are these that Cairo is often called the "City of a Thousand Minarets".

It is also said that "Man fears time but time fears the Pyramids". The spectacular sound-and-light show at the pyramids, the artistic presentations producing an inspiring, almost romantic atmosphere, tells the story of the building of the pyramids. The Egyptian museum is one of the world's greatest. But for me, the glory of Egypt was to be found in its ancient monuments — pharonic, Christian and Islamic — some preserved for as long as 7,000 years by the extremely dry climate.

24 February 1985

On to Luxor, 600 miles south of Cairo by overnight sleeper train "where stones are more precious than gold", the location of the pharaohs' Winter Palace. This city on the Nile, the centre of Egyptian power, glory and life, is often referred to as the world's greatest outdoor museum. Nowhere else in the world has time left such a great wealth of ancient civilisation.

We stayed in a colonial-style hotel with a view of the Nile. On the terraced bar, we watched the sunset over the river's west bank and its famed Valley of the Kings and Queens. It was an elegant retreat, set amidst one of the oldest recorded civilisations known to humanity. We indulged in a drink for every *felucca* which sailed by.

On the east bank are the statues and columns of the Temples of Luxor and Karnac. On the west bank lies Tutankhamun's tomb in the City of the Dead, the valley of the Kings and Queens, and the impressive mortuary temple of Queen Hatsherput. Egypt is a land of mystery where one can feel the almost unimaginable power of the pharaohs.

01 March 1985

Enough Egyptian culture: it was time to relax, really relax. We headed north to the legendary Land of Plenty, flowing with milk and honey, to Israel's sparkling Red Sea jewel, the seaside resort of Eilat. Here we relaxed in the winter sunshine and sampled culture of a different kind, most of which we found to be American in style… but we could live with that.

It was both warm and sunny. The hotel's swimming pool attendant had a preference for playing tapes whose smooth, soothing style was terrifically therapeutic. So we spent a blissful sun-drenched week of swimming, sipping beer, and "Shalom". Inevitably, leave ended too quickly, and it was time to venture northwards, travelling the full length of Israel. One full day, two buses and a taxi journey brought us to the Lebanese border and a return to cold reality. With a sinking feeling of near dread in the pit of our stomachs, neither was looking forward to facing the inevitable tension, confrontations and trouble.

Greeted with news of a further deterioration in the operational situation, we were not happy. "Cheer up... ye'll laugh about it some day" came the cheery greeting of the convoy commander taking us back to our respective company areas. His remarks unwittingly reassured us that whatever we'd have to face, we would not be doing so alone — wasn't there a whole battalion of Irishmen with us?

IN THE COCKPIT

09 March 1985

With the gentle arrival of spring, the first noticeable change was the light-green moss-like covering of new grasses that appeared everywhere. This was quickly followed by large patches of earth-hugging blue and mauve flowers, the crocuses. As the spring heat intensified, a profusion of colours carpeted the landscape. Here and there overhead, the brilliant whites and pinks of the cherry blossoms added to this palette of colour and rebirth.

As the plants began to burst forth, so also did the animal life. Everywhere little mounds of fresh earth were being pushed up in almost straight lines. These were the moles, opening up new tunnels and chambers as they looked for roots and underground shoots to eat. The reptiles also began to awaken from their winter hibernation, and next to emerge were the lizards and geckos. These four-legged long-tailed creatures came out when the sun had heated up the rocks that formed their winter homes. They could be seen basking on the stones as they waited for passing insects which they attacked with a speed that was difficult to follow.

High up, the spring migration of birds had begun. White storks, eagles, buzzards, kites, hawks and falcons trickled northwards as they soared and glided on the thermals, conserving their energies for the long journeys to their nesting areas. There was a sudden influx of small birds bush-hopping and feeding on the lush, new greenery as they winged their way north.

Also high above was the deep, humming sound of Israeli army drones, diminutive unpiloted aircraft used to survey the

topography of Lebanon. Their presence characterised the
increased tension in the area of operations. The Israeli army
and its security services carried out searches or snatches of
suspect persons, surrounding villages and removing some of
their youths and men for interrogation. Roadside bombs and
suicide bomb attacks became the standard reaction from the
Lebanese Shia Amal and Hezbullah activists. As the Israeli army
withdrew southwards, so these activities moved with them.

The question in most people's minds was where the Israeli
army would establish a new enclave line in the south. Clearly
the existing line was, in many areas, tactically unsound. This
question had ominous implications for the Irish battalion since
its area contained key terrain features on which Israeli military
and surveillance positions could be sited. This surveillance
sector would extend over six villages and reach the next ridgeline, the Jebel Amal, on which Tibnin and the Irish battalion's
headquarters were located. Emphasis was placed on the need
for even greater security and readiness as it was evident that
tension would rise in the wake of the Israeli army's close
concentration on the villages adjacent to the enclave.

While this important issue was yet to develop, the final
inter-platoon rotations occurred. My platoon left the village
hot spot and assumed responsibility for three locations in the
company area immediately adjacent to the enclave. I
wondered whether we were going from the heat into the fire.

One of these locations, a hill-top observation post,
occupied the second most important terrain feature in the
Irish battalion area. It was sure to be of interest to the Israeli
army. The observation post and nearby checkpoint, although
some distance apart, worked in tandem in maintaining a
check on the movement of vehicles leaving the enclave and
entering the Irish battalion area. The UN's standard operating
procedures did not permit these movements to be refused
entry into the UN zone once we established that *bona fide*,
card-carrying members of the Israeli army security services
were present. The majority of these card numbers and their
holders soon became known to the Irish. It was not unknown,

however, for the Christian militia forces to use these identification cards to gain entry into the Irish battalion area.

Checking these card-holders was a daily occurrence. Extreme vigilance was required, regardless of the size and make-up of the movements or the mood and intent of the personnel. When necessary, entry was denied by establishing a stop gap, with an Irish armoured personnel carrier blocking the roadway. Especially constructed tank stops were pushed onto the roadway; checkpoints were reinforced; and the company reserve was put on standby to assist if the situation deteriorated.

As soldiers, we often wondered at the wisdom — or lack of it — which permitted armed Israeli Shin Bet intelligence men to pass through UN checkpoints. It might be said that there was no alternative. Plain-clothes Israeli intelligence operatives could pass through with Israeli military patrols if they wished — and they sometimes did, although making specific exception for these men was a disturbing precedent. Their activities inside the area of operations in other battalion areas often involved conflict with the local populations, undercover arrests, and unexplained shooting incidents. Should UN policy give these men access to the area of operations, it was not something which on-the-ground peacekeepers were free to interpret. Instead, we found that it was better to focus on what we could achieve, and the Irish battalion's presence was undoubtedly causing problems for the Israeli army.

Behind both the present and the new enclave lines, the Israeli army did not want impartial European troops watching their behaviour, monitoring their movements and trying to establish the sovereignty of the Lebanese government in an area in which the Israeli army wanted their own militias to hold sway. Thus firing on Irish troops became a near nightly occurrence.

18 March 1985

Firing was not confined to the night, however. One afternoon, returning to the post which now housed our platoon headquarters, I jumped out of my jeep and nodded towards Sergeant Paddy who had been anxiously awaiting my arrival. One look at the expression on my face told him that the inspection for which we had been preparing for weeks had gone well. A member of the general staff on a four-day visit from Ireland had found no cause for adverse comment and was full of praise. The effort involved in the preparations had paid off and the general's satisfaction should have justified a period of relative relaxation.

Hardly had Sergeant Paddy returned my knowing glance when the sound of gunfire from the nearby village interrupted our moment of triumph. The increasing intensity of the fire suggested a degree of intent which warranted concern, caution, but most of all, action. Jumping back into the jeep, the experience of four months' peacekeeping made me order the checkpoint party to accompany me. Whatever situation we were going to find was better faced with an immediate force of numbers, rather than seeking reinforcements later. As the jeep sped off, Sergeant Paddy was already organising the now alerted post personnel in anticipation of a confrontation, unaware of how protracted it would become.

At the nearest containing checkpoint, the five Irish sentries had all taken cover behind sandbagged positions. Sentries at the village checkpoint, concerned by the ever-increasing rate of fire, were greatly relieved by the quick arrival of reinforcements. It wasn't hard to grasp the severity of the fire, so on reaching the checkpoint, we ourselves were not slow in taking cover. This high rate of fire had been directed mainly at the other Irish checkpoint in the village. A few moments beforehand, a local gang member, Josef Almaz (known to us all as "Jimi Hendrix" due to his close resemblance to the singer), had been refused passage for failing to submit his car to a search. He returned to his house and opened fire with a light machine gun.

The gunfire started fast, then accelerated. Supporting fire came from a number of houses on the militia side of the village. Under their formidable local henchman, Nabbi, the

The author, Commandant Dan Harvey, on one of his tours with UNIFIL.

The Crusader castle, Toron, dominates the village of Tibnin where Irish UNIFIL troops were deployed.

"Camp Shamrock", home of Ireland's UNIFIL forces, with the Norwegian Maintenance Company HQ in the background.

The UN flag flies over a UNIFIL checkpoint.

Irish peacekeepers on checkpoint duty.

An Israeli Merkava tank and crew, part of a mobile patrol in the Irish Battalion Area of Operations.

Ancient and modern: An elderly Lebanese villager sets the pace.

UNIFIL Humanitarian Aid: An Irish medic with an old village woman at the At-Tiri clinic.

militiamen were giving full vent to their propensity for violence and exercising little or no restraint. The situation was serious and dangerous.

It was time to get the other checkpoint personnel to a more secure position, and they were ordered to move back to the shelter of a building behind them as darkness fell. In the village, the Irish inside the post known as the CO's house, recently the headquarters of our platoon, returned fire over the heads of the attackers to cover the withdrawal of the checkpoint personnel. The noise of the gunfire, its immediacy, the colours of the tracer rounds, the constant crackle of radio traffic, the controlled urgency in the voice and the economic use of words — all gave rise to a mingling of fear and fascination.

Such feelings were momentary, however, as the situation was well beyond allowing ourselves to be caught wrong-footed; precise concentration was required. This confrontation was our most menacing and testing to date, with the already heavy rate of incoming gunfire intensifying. It was somehow curious to be so totally immersed in the hostilities, mind racing, anticipating, yet simultaneously, almost involuntarily, making specific observations. I was struck by how automatic our movements were, textbook reaction drills of cover and manoeuvre complemented by skilful weapon handling, crisp, smart and purposeful. I sensed a confidence and a determination, a no-nonsense demeanour, and a mind-set that was both forthright and disciplined. We had received our baptism of fire the day after our arrival in the village. The platoon's character was further forged in the succeeding incident-filled and tense two months and was now going through its most testing crucible to date, an all-out fire fight. The response of even the first-time, inexperienced soldiers was now that of mature peacekeepers, for that is what they had become. They were performing to the required, long-practised standards which were impressive to witness in action.

Suddenly, a flash of bright light exploded from behind the militia checkpoint, temporarily illuminating their house, the roadway and all the immediate area. It was the signature flash and smoke discharge of an RPG-7 rocket anti-tank grenade launcher. Almost simultaneously, the thunder from the blast of its impact detonation pierced our ears. We all froze. This was not Kilworth, Kilbride, the Glen of Imaal, the Curragh or any other army practice range we'd ever been on. This was no exercise. We were face to face with the reality, and fragility, of our lives. It is said of soldiering that you don't know your profession until you have come under fire for real, an initiation which has no equivalent in any other walk of life.

The rocket blasted into the side of a house twenty yards in front of the platoon headquarters. Another rocket cleared the top of the building. The rounds from the crackling chatter of their heavy machine gun lent an artificial brilliance to the scene. The tracer paths could be tracked by their orange-red trails as the rounds arced onto their target. They were firing for effect, intent on killing, while we were directing "suppressing fire" over their heads to hinder their aim.

In the midst of this turmoil, noise and high drama, I heard our company commander radio his request that the AML-90 armoured car commander, part of the battalion's mobile reserve, be brought up to assist us; he also wanted to know the exact type of ammunition available to him. This request for increased fire-power was as reassuring as it was sudden, as logical as it was shocking. We were encouraged by the availability of this extra fire-power and the fact that our commander was considering using it. For the time being, our own light arms and the light machine gun on the roof of the platoon headquarters would make our reply.

The firing continued for almost two full hours before ceasing; they had obviously exhausted themselves. At midnight, we took advantage of the lull to rotate fresh troops onto our checkpoint and rest those who had been involved in the hostilities from the beginning. The platoon commanders remained overnight for continuity and reassurance, available immediately should the situation erupt again.

19 March 1985

At dawn, the Irish reoccupied their checkpoint. A little later in the morning, the second part of the bizarre saga commenced as we heard the footsteps of children and elderly people moving through the village, congregating at the militiamen's house. It was strange, even eerie, that they neither spoke to nor looked at the Irish as they passed, their normal spontaneity frozen by fear. A few moments later, their intended use became apparent. The villagers were being forced to advance on both Irish checkpoints simultaneously, the children towards the village centre, the elderly towards the outer checkpoint. The militiamen remained behind them, shouting abuse and cocking their weapons. They were being used as human shields in the take-over of the checkpoints.

The situation demanded an immediate reaction. Seconds counted and lives were in jeopardy. The checkpoint troops were withdrawn in good order, quickly salvaging all equipment. The checkpoints were overrun. The village checkpoint party withdrew into the platoon headquarters' house. I quickly selected a house which afforded good observation into the checkpoint and good protection in the event of yet another Israeli army pressure tactic being used in this difficult episode. Fortunately, the house was vacant. Here again, the ordered withdrawal was affected by using cover and manoeuvre drill... basic tactics, perhaps, but the training was coming to the fore. So too was the disciplined restraint for which the Irish were known.

The situation was tense. In the village square, the school children were now throwing stones, eggs and whatever else at the platoon headquarters, laying siege to it, urged on by the militia gang to become a marauding mob. The Irish inside simply waited for the children to run out of eggs and stones. Meanwhile, the militia was attempting to dismantle the checkpoints.

During incidents, it was standard practice for the UN to contact the Israeli defence forces' liaison officer which usually had the effect of normalising the situation. During the previous night's shooting, a local response from the Israelis did occur and the militia gang was allegedly ordered to stop. It was subsequent to that, however, that the second rocket was fired. This time, a senior Israeli liaison officer arrived and negotiations began with the Irish battalion commander. Eventually, after many hours of straight talking, the situation was resolved and it was agreed that the checkpoints were to be returned. The militia gang was slow to leave them, however, and the tension lingered. Eventually, and with great care, we were able to reoccupy the checkpoints. It was time for the platoon commanders to get some sleep.

20 March 1985

The following day, Nabbi, the village gang leader, was speaking with the village platoon commander, Captain Pat Winters from Carlow. As was often the way of things, Nabbi changed personality mid-sentence and strutted off, making threats. Life had returned to normal. So had the platoon's sense of humour. It was decided that it must have been "Jimi Hendrix", our "cross-eyed militiaman", who had been firing the rocket-propelled grenade launcher — when aiming, he was obviously closing the wrong eye.

QUICKSAND

Like most countries in the region, Lebanon had survived numerous invasions throughout its long history, many of which had left traces on the landscape. Scattered throughout the land are many castles from Crusader times when a series of military expeditions, commencing in the late eleventh century and extending over a 200-year period, were made by western Christians seeking to free the Holy Land from Muslim domination. Surrounded with an aura of romance and chivalry, grandeur and gallantry, this has more to do with legend than historical fact.

While the Crusaders had made many conquests, they did not permanently free the Holy Land. Tibnin, Irish battalion headquarters, was selected for the Crusader fortress which dominated the surrounding countryside and controlled the route from Jerusalem to Tyre. Called Toron, from the old French word meaning "turret" or "high place", the castle stands atop a rounded hill which determined the shape of the fortifications.

Eighty years after it was established, the great Muslim and political leader, Saladin, consolidated his power throughout Egypt and extended his control over Syria. He then inflicted a decisive defeat over the Crusaders and went on to recapture Jerusalem. Saladin's nephew next led a large force to capture Toron in Tibnin. So overawed was he by the size of the fortifications that he claimed it could not be captured without Saladin himself.

Saladin made ready to do battle, but to his great surprise, the French Crusaders surrendered without a fight, although they subsequently made fruitless efforts to recapture the castle. Since Crusader times, Toron has been much disputed, attacked, rebuilt and again destroyed. All that remains from then is the substructure of large dressed blocks which are still in position to the west and in front of the enclosure wall. Long-suffering and much occupied by many invading armies, Toron, like Lebanon itself, has witnessed the wars of the world with all their associated horror and brutality. Following the Israeli invasion and reinvasion of South Lebanon, some units of the Israeli army who were in Tibnin used Toron as an observation post.

Now that the Israeli army's phased withdrawal had gathered considerable momentum, such "high places" would be key terrain and very much in demand, particularly the dominating ridge of hills immediately adjacent, but significantly forward, of the present Christian enclave line. Affording spectacular views northwards across the stony, barren valleys towards Tibnin, this ridgeline was critical military terrain which had to be held. The problem was that the Irish battalion already had observation posts along it.

The highest of these hills was the responsibility of our neighbouring company. However, the ridgeline extended into our company area and the second highest hill was one of our platoon's responsibilities. For the Israelis, a militarily stronger and extended enclave line must surely encompass both hilltop positions. Debates on the issue ended when Israeli helicopters and M113 armoured personnel carriers moved onto the highest of the hills. It could only be a matter of time before the new enclave line was established.

For now, though, happenings lower down our hill on the roadway checkpoint were the focus of the platoon's attention, given an increase in military traffic both coming from and going to the enclave. This checkpoint had been established when the Irish first joined the UN force in June 1978. Its purpose was to monitor and control all traffic entering and leaving the UN area from the south, as well as to prevent pro-Israeli Christian militia and the Israeli army from entering the area. The checkpoint also acted as an early-warning of any approaching vehicles. Originally manned by one corporal and one private, it was now reinforced by an AML-90 armoured car with a crew of two. This was later withdrawn and replaced by an armoured personnel carrier and bofors 90mm anti-tank gun and crew. A bomb shelter was erected which could accommodate the two corporals and four privates.

This checkpoint had always seen a lot of action, including attempted incursions by the Christian militia and the Israeli army. Using half-track vehicles, the Christian militia would approach at speed, often firing as they approached. They would withdraw when the AML-90 armoured car appeared on the road. When this was replaced by the armoured personnel carrier, the militia often rammed it when it was used as a stop gap.

The Israeli-backed Christian militia opened fire on the checkpoint without provocation. It was also subjected to shelling and tank fire originating from further within the enclave.

Although traffic along the road had returned to a slow but steady flow, recent months had witnessed an increase in Israeli army and pro-Israeli militia movements passing through the checkpoint and giving rise to both near and actual incidents. Increasingly, we began to see Israeli army convoys withdrawing southwards, concurrent with smaller Israeli Shin Bet intelligence agents' movements northwards. Their activities north of the Irish battalion were ostensibly to counter resistance in the villages in order to secure the Israeli army routes of withdrawal; an army is never more vulnerable than when it is in retreat. Witnessing the size of some of these withdrawing convoys and the battle-worn demeanour of their occupants, we had to wonder at what dynamic had forced this once-feared army to flee... Lebanon had become Israel's Vietnam. They entered Lebanon to rid it of Palestinian guerrillas and became locked in a conflict with the Lebanese themselves, both civilian and guerrillas. Used to fighting and winning an all-out war of short duration, they now found themselves in the unfamiliar role of an occupying army. Israel had become an aggressor. The Israeli army found itself in a quagmire and was experiencing its first defeat.

Due to the increased significance which this checkpoint had assumed in vetting movements from the enclave, it was increased in size and fortified by an earthen-bank surround, similar to an Israeli army position, with rolls of barbed wire, sand-bagged positions and gabions, wire-meshed cages filled with rocks and stones. Its new look served to increase its potential as a focal point for trouble. Its complement had also been increased and as platoon commander, I was located there full-time.

The checkpoint's fortification works had commenced before our platoon's arrival and we now continued them in earnest. Equally in earnest were the attempts by Israeli-backed Christian militiamen to gain entry through this checkpoint without the due authority vested in the recognised pass cards. Our firmness in refusing such attempts was consistent, although never heavy-handed. It became a daily battle of wits and nerves as we combated their attempts at subterfuge, threats and intimidation.

One morning, Nabbi arrived at the checkpoint from the enclave with what appeared to be a woman passenger… only it wasn't. It was another infamous militia gang leader from the Irish battalion's other hot spot. He wore a wig at a feeble attempt of disguise. Our orders were that neither of these men should be allowed into our area, whether alone or together, so entry was refused. Loss of face or not, especially for the one with the makeup, they were not allowed to pass.

As might have been expected, this denial of entry did not spark an incident. Instead they laughed it off and returned to the enclave… perhaps they were getting giddy. I certainly noticed a degree of giddiness among my own platoon, putting shoe polish and golden syrup on the lenses of each other's binoculars, amongst other practical jokes. This air of light-headedness was mainly due to the news that our relief battalion had been activated at home; it was forming up and commencing preparatory training. The names of our replacements were known, a small but significant landmark in its own right.

30 March 1985

There was still plenty to occupy our minds, much of it causing grave concern. Information had filtered through that six more rocket-propelled grenade-launchers had been issued to the militia gangs. Of a more sinister nature, news arrived that all males between the ages of seventeen and twenty-five were liable to be press-ganged into these village militias. The village *mukhtars* or headmen had been ordered to collect "taxes" to pay for this increased village "protection"; they were being forced to pay for their own oppressors. Should they refuse, they could expect trouble. Militia gangs would come from other villages, and any men who were then inmates of the notorious prison and torture camps would not be released until they agreed to pay.

02 April 1985

A few mornings later as I was about to visit the third of the platoon's locations, I was standing at the checkpoint and witnessed the routine search of a car driven by one of the militia gang. Thinking no more of the affair and having mounted the jeep, my driver and I began our journey and were surprised, then alarmed, to find that the militiaman had done a U-turn and was in fact giving chase. He was blowing his car horn in an effort to attract the attention of the Christian militiamen who had a checkpoint on the crossroads which we had to negotiate in order to arrive at another of our platoon's positions. This particular crossroads was the gateway to the Christian militia enclave.

It was a predicament. We were closing on the militia checkpoint and he was closing on us. I looked at my driver, Private Billy Harris, a tough, witty, intensely loyal soldier from the north of Cork City. He read my mind and put his foot down. Unfortunately for us, we had to take a 90° turn at the crossroads and so had to slow down. The revving of the jeep's engine as we changed down gears did not drown out the persistent horn-blowing of our pursuer. The best we could hope for was that the sentries on the checkpoint were slack.

I looked hard at Private Harris and told him calmly: "I don't think we should stop!" With equal calm, he replied: "I don't think so either, Sir!" We didn't.

At their own checkpoint, the militia sentries were not on the roadway proper. Taking full advantage of their casualness, we waved politely and drove through at speed until, much relieved, we reached our own checkpoint just beyond the crossroads.

The incident didn't end there, however. So fired up was our pursuer that he followed us all the way through the checkpoint. With the scales now tipped in our favour, I could negotiate with him from a position of strength to find out what was bothering him. I was conscious of not losing face in front of my own men, but without creating problems further down the road either.

It turned out that the militia leader had taken exception to submitting his car to the routine search. Annoyed and volatile, he had given chase and was now threatening "big trouble" if it happened again. I told him calmly but firmly that it would, and that I was going to inform "my friend" Nabbi about the matter. His temperament immediately changed and, making face-saving threats, he got into his car and sped off. I was glad we had had this exchange at our checkpoint and not at the crossroads. It's amazing the difference a hundred yards of ground can make. But then, this was South Lebanon, and it was all about ground, and occupying it.

The ground surrounding this checkpoint and post was adjacent to a village which, in the early years of the UN, had been the hot spot of the Irish battalion. The Christian militia had entered the village from the enclave with a tank, a half-track and a number of light vehicles. They then set up a checkpoint at the crossroads and built a small tank compound on the western side of the village. Negotiations failed to get them to withdraw. They established a permanent post and fired regularly on the surrounding villages. The Irish were constantly sending reports of these firings to UNIFIL operations cell.

Although the militia had tried to break through the Irish positions in the direction of Tibnin and Bra'shit on a number of occasions, they had failed because the post had two armoured personnel carriers and an AML-90 armoured car attached to it. Thus the crossroads became the centre for negotiations between the Irish and the Christian militia. Although the UNIFIL mandate was to confirm the departure of the Israeli army, members of this force were regularly spotted in the village, training the Christian militia in the use of weapons and issuing rations. The post continued to be a flash point for the Irish until the Israeli army reinvaded Lebanon. They then removed their tank and half-track and the post became less prominent and less tense. But now, it was once again the focus for confrontation.

Typical of Lebanon, events had come full circle. With its latest invaders in full retreat, tension had returned to the area. As the battalion neared the end of its tour, it seemed obvious that the operational situation was going to become even more tense. It was unfortunate that the advance party of our relieving battalion would soon arrive and be greeted by a worsening situation. It was also becoming clear that the attempted creation of a *cordon-sanitaire* would become part of the more extended enclave. The all-important ground we occupied was becoming quicksand. Yet we resolved to respond forthrightly and steadfastly to Israeli pressure tactics. We were going to stand firm in this quagmire.

CRITICAL TERRAIN

09 April 1985

Soldiers on parade attract attention. The sharpness of their response to shouted orders, be it arms or foot drill, is impressive. The exact timing and smartness of their movements display a crisp cohesiveness and interdependence that is out of the ordinary. The special "soldier-like" quality suggests an underlying seriousness and competence, as well as an understated pride in their integrity and identity. The larger the parade, the more graphic the impression.

The Ministerial Review and March-Past of the entire battalion immediately prior to its rotation to Lebanon was impressive. Now, five months later, it was time to parade again as a battalion, with the "first-timers" receiving their overseas service medal, a decoration awarded to those who were performing peacekeeping duties in Lebanon. Presented by the UN force commander, the recipients feel a distinct sense of pride at this embellishment, universally recognised as a symbol of service of worth, and individually valued.

The accompanying military parade formed the centrepiece of a showcased Irish National Day when the battalion played host to its UN neighbours, celebrating its identity as only the Irish can. The parading soldiers exemplified the strong sense of discipline, loyalty and teamwork which are synonymous with the military. Their training engendered a commitment to military service which implied an acceptance of the unusual, the irregular, and the sometimes stressful and life-threatening. This resulted in soldiers, now peacekeepers, who had been trained to operate with professionalism in difficult, tense and dangerous situations. As the cruel reality of the guerrilla war in Lebanon edged nearer, they were increasingly relied upon to carry out a variety of peacekeeping tasks even when it meant potential risk to life and limb.

16 April 1985
"619 Charlie", the platoon's hilltop observation post, maintained all-round surveillance of the southern part of the Irish battalion's area of operations and had good views south towards the enclave. It was from here that I received a report just before three o'clock one morning that a large Israeli army force was on the move northwards into the Irish battalion area. This was not going to be good news for someone somewhere. The concentration of Israeli armoured fighting vehicles suggested a cordon-and-search operation; it was unlikely to be executed without violence.

I contacted company headquarters and advised them that there was "a bit of work" on the way for one of our neighbouring companies and had the message relayed through battalion operations cell, alerting all Irish posts and making ready the mobile reserve. Within minutes, the outlying section and platoon posts were confirming their approach.

Initially, ten Israeli intelligence service vehicles, fifteen M113 armoured personnel carriers, ten trucks, four half-trucks, two Range Rovers, two ambulances and eight jeeps made up the Israeli movement. Eventually, fifty-eight vehicles with approximately 300 Israeli army, intelligence and their various militias' personnel entered the village of Yatar. They blocked off the access roads and tracks. Already alerted, and with predetermined resolve, three Irish battalion armoured personnel carriers attempted to gain admittance to the village. Two were initially blocked but the third managed to move up a back track and gained access to the village. After discussions, bluffs and threats, the other armoured personnel carriers was also able to enter the village. One took up position at the graveyard, the other on the high ground overlooking the waterhole. The company duty officer, too,

had his route to the village blocked by an Israeli M113, so he
and his driver manhandled their radio set into the centre of
the village and took up a rooftop position overlooking the
school yard.

Meanwhile, the Israelis and their militias took up position
throughout the village, rounding up all the local men above
the age of sixteen who were brought to the lower hall of the
schoolhouse for interrogation. When they had all the men,
they sent out search teams to check the houses. While this
was taking place, the hugely outnumbered Irish were being
confronted with many difficult situations. The two rooftop
observers were confronted by about twenty militia gang
members who pushed them about, threatening them with
knives and cocking their weapons. The crews of the Irish
armoured personnel carriers which had courageously broken
the Israeli cordon were themselves besieged by highly
aggressive militiamen, also cocking their weapons and
threatening them with grenades with their pins pulled out.

The Irish stood their ground unflinchingly, absorbing the
aggression, refusing to be intimidated. Eventually, an Israeli
officer ordered the militiamen off the roof and away from the
Irish. Meanwhile, the Irish company commander, a battalion
commander and a group of UNIFIL headquarters officers from
Naquora were refused entry to the village. They were
physically abused and pushed about and had weapons cocked
at them. They nonetheless gained entry to the village on foot
to monitor the Israeli activity. During the morning's events, a
number of UN vehicles were damaged and many personnel
threatened. Their element of surprise lost, their activities
disrupted and their presence monitored, the main Israeli party
left the village mid-morning. A demolition crew remained and
demolished five buildings with controlled explosions, then
withdrew.

We interpreted this operation as a prelude to another
objective: the pursuit of high ground and critical terrain. The
prospect of the area's attempted occupation by the Israelis was
growing nearer and nearer. In the event, it was almost

immediate. Later that same evening, two Israeli M113 armoured personnel carriers escorted a huge civilian bulldozer from the enclave towards Hill 880. It was obvious that the Israelis were making their long-awaited bid.

The battalion mobile reserve was again activated and sent to Hill 880 to monitor the Israeli army movements from there. The Israelis moved onto the hilltop and their presence was protested. Before five the next morning, the bulldozer commenced work, which was protested by the platoon commander. The work ceased, but resumed again after an hour. When this happened again, the full battalion mobile reserve was activated and the company reconnaissance section's armoured personnel carriers were employed to stop the bulldozer. The Israelis offered no resistance, emphasising that they wanted no argument with the UN. Irish troops were out on the ground to stop the work, but the bulldozer's sheer size managed to create earthen embankments between itself and the armoured personnel carriers and continued its work. Two more Irish armoured personnel carriers arrived but they could not negotiate the embankments; the bulldozer could work for substantial periods without obstruction. Through persistence, however, one Irish armoured personnel carrier managed to break the embankment and occupy the perimeter. A new Irish UN post was established there.

Now midday, the situation grew tense and the company was advised not to enter into a physical confrontation — the Irish UN troops would have to be pushed off their post rather than leave.

* * *

Further obstruction of the Israelis was inappropriate, so by the end of the day's events, both the Israelis and the Irish occupied the same post around which a 10-feet-high earth embankment had been constructed. This situation continued for a number of days, during which time the Israelis abandoned their position on the Harris-Haddatha road after a

tank arrived and escorted their personnel away. The local Irish
platoon then sent a foot patrol to the area and found it strewn
with ammunition, unconsumed rations and debris.

This "coexistence" atop Hill 880 ceased two days later
when the UN force commander instructed that the UN could
not be seen to be in joint occupation of a post with another
belligerent; a new UN post would have to be established. It
was into the midst of this volatile situation that the advance
party of the new Irish battalion arrived. Comprising the
battalion commander and his staff officers, their presence
marked a new era. It was both unusual and welcoming to see
their new unit's flash insignia.

The Israelis finally began to withdraw. A new enclave line
or security zone was established which overlapped parts of the
Irish battalion's area. Hill 880 was now occupied by the
Israelis: "619 Charlie" was next. It would soon be time to go
to work ourselves. We were earning our peacekeeping medals
the hard way.

BETWEEN THE LINES

"Man down! Man down! Med evac! Med evac!"

Platoons and their commanders dreaded hearing these words over the radio, reporting a serious casualty and requesting a medical evacuation. Conscious of maintaining a twenty-four-hour "listening watch", radio traffic was continuously monitored as a matter of course and had become second nature to us all. As well as providing a vital communications and reporting link, the radio net served to make post commanders feel less isolated.

The responsibility of commanding a platoon dispersed between separate locations in a highly volatile area at a crucial time was becoming increasingly onerous. Rank has its responsibilities and its roles, and concern for the platoon's security is felt acutely by those charged with ensuring their safety and welfare. The corporal section commander and his second-in-command, deployed as checkpoint commanders, had the difficult task of being the front-line decision-makers. It was their judgment, their decision, their call in the first instance which mattered. Their initial actions and reactions allowed platoon commanders room for manoeuvre, allowing a negotiated resolution once a confrontation or other problem had commenced. These checkpoint teams were relied upon heavily and had discharged their tasks with common sense and courage. The experience which the platoon had gained since our arrival, especially in the last four months, had required them to produce that combination of qualities best distinguished as character. A sense of family, of belonging, had evolved. This held us together when the going got hectic. There was an unspoken loyalty, a respect of and appreciation for each other's role and an easy camaraderie. This, then, was both the responsibility and reward of rank, the two sides of the same coin. As platoon commander, I could not allow a lapse of confidence or concentration, particularly as the handover to the newly arriving battalion was imminent. Traditionally, this was often a period fraught with danger when interested parties sought to take advantage of the new battalion's unfamiliarity with terrain, procedures, person-alities and now, a new, complex and constantly changing status quo.

* * *

Red Range Rovers, orange Volkswagen vans... the type, make and colour of Israeli defence force reconnaissance vehicles were varied and numerous, but their intention was clear and single-minded: "619 Charlie" was firmly in their sights. Despite the landmark events of the last week — the Israeli army's presence on Hill 880 and the air of inevitability about their arrival to our hill — the detail of our required reactions was no less real or dramatic. The uncertainty and fluidity of the general operational situation, while not lessening the pace for a second, was becoming more fixed, with less confused lines of demarcation. An apparent frontline was evolving.

We had witnessed the commencement of the process: our limited time would mean that we would not see it resolved. A retreating Israeli army under increasing attack, the creation of a new enclave line, the repression of the indigenous Lebanese population — the Irish battalion area was where these forces met and merged, resulting in a cauldron, a testing crucible for peace and those charged with keeping it: us.

This operational situation had pushed peacekeeping to its limits, the increasing aggressiveness constantly challenging the soldier as peacekeeper to control and contain the violence. Each new, heightened circumstance followed closely on the last heated exchange and forced the peacekeeper to adapt constantly. The Irish had become adept at adapting, and quickly. They responded with appropriate brinkmanship, utilising an intelligent mix of firmness yet adherence to UN policy.

24 April 1985

The arrival of Chalk One of our replacement battalion was a welcome event. Over a third were arriving on the ground, the corresponding number of our battalion having rotated home. The close-knit integrity of our battalion and its sub-units, my platoon included, had been broken. Chalk One's imminent arrival caused us to reinterpret our situation through the eyes of the newcomers. What had become ordinary, everyday and commonplace for us would be extraordinary for them. They had to hit the ground running, and it was up to us to give them all the help we could.

It was both unfortunate and typical, then, that the first of our platoon replacements arrived at the very moment when two Israeli jet fighters flew low overhead, shattering both the sound barrier and their nerves with a thunderous clap from the sonic booms. Conscious not to do the "old soldier", I left any philosophising out and offered only one bit of advice to my replacement: "It gets even better." In the event, the old army adage of "learning by doing" came into play sooner than I had anticipated. That night, the Israelis on Hill 880 lit up the sky with flares and fired into the surrounding waddies, fearful of any infiltration attacks by Amal and Hezbullah fighters, setting the pattern for what remained of our tour.

27 April 1985

Shortly after Chalk One's arrival, our observation post on 619 Charlie reported an Israeli army movement of three vehicles approaching from the enclave. Monitored from a long way off, the checkpoint personnel routinely prepared for the vehicles' arrival, no doubt seeking passage through the checkpoint. Well used to seeing many kinds of Israeli army vehicle movements, the combination of one M113, a half-track, and a silver BMW saloon was not an unusual configuration in itself.

Nonetheless, the checkpoint commander felt that something was amiss; it warranted closer attention, and the matter was reported to the platoon sergeant.

Still some distance away, the vehicles' high rate of speed and large numbers of occupants, both in and on each vehicle, was disquieting. Alerted by the platoon sergeant, it was time for me to "walk slowly while thinking quickly" onto the roadway checkpoint. I contemplated ordering our armoured personnel carrier across the road, but instead, I opted for a low-key approach and remained on the roadway with Sergeant Paddy. We decided to halt the lead vehicle, the M113 full-track, in the normal way, but it showed no signs of slowing. It was then I noticed that both of the notorious village militia leaders were among the occupants. They appeared, as did all their companions, hyped up to the last. Now nearer, there was a perceptible wildness, almost a brutal recklessness, about them which bore all the hallmarks of a mischief-making sortie. We were to be their first stop... if they actually stopped.

Despite the fact that we were clearly visible in the centre of the road, the driver of the M113 paid no attention to my upraised hand and did not slow his pace. Not to move would be madness, yet to do so would somehow be a defeat. This was not grand-standing for the sake of those newly arrived, but an expression which gave effect to the principle of minimum force — a microcosm of the entire peacekeeping effort — by literally standing up to intimidation.

Options were being lost by the second. It was fast approaching commitment point, that threshold when the driver of the lead vehicle would either have to slow or be unable to slow in time to avoid us. But there was no sign of deceleration. It was a matter of wills and a matter of pride.

Soldiers are human, and the front page of my local news-paper at home, with the headline "Peacekeepers flattened", flashed into my mind and curiously fortified my faltering courage as an idea struck me.

"We're moving," I said.

"We're not, Sir," came Sergeant Paddy's reply. "At least not backwards, or sideways — but forward. He won't be expecting that."

He smiled a satisfied smile and together, we took three paces forward.

It *was* the last thing the driver expected, and his sheer reflex reaction brought the M113 to a sudden, jerky halt, causing it to veer sideways amid a cloud of dirt, dust and debris. We were almost deafened, not by the noise of the skid but by the cheers of the platoon members, both new and old. It was a chastening experience but we'd won. At least it was a kind of victory in a typical cat-and-mouse situation, playing out a deeper conflict and testing our level of resolve. It was important to remind them of the fact.

A valid identification card was produced by an accredited Israeli military cardholder and the movement was allowed to proceed. Two days later, they came for 619 Charlie.

29 April 1985

The long-awaited move finally came. Initially, two Israeli jeeps and two M113s came forward to secure the hill. For soldiers, holding the ground — particularly high ground and especially key terrain which granted you an advantage — was crucial. Conventional military tactics, our favoured option, was to defend the hill with all available manpower and weapons until it became untenable. But we were peacekeepers, and not looking for enemies. Our skills were employed to accomplish a worthwhile peace, but this was to be achieved on the sidelines of someone else's war: we were simply to protest the Israeli army presence on the hill. We did so by putting a coil of barbed wire across the track near the summit and, along with my platoon's occupants of the observation post, we stood shoulder-to-shoulder behind it to deny the Israelis access.

The commander of the leading M113 looked at us incredulously, as we knew he would. Talking into his headset, he ordered the driver to bypass us and take up positions on the hill's north-facing summit. There, they were joined by two huge bulldozers which immediately set to work in earnest, building a massive earth-embankment compound.

Within a week, the second chalk rotated, the Israeli withdrawal continued, and we had handed over full operational control to the "new" Irish battalion five years to the day on which I had been commissioned. Lebanon had taught me several lessons. I was the better for the experience, and there were three things of which I was profoundly certain: it had been difficult, physically tough, physiologically taxing and at times dangerous; it was worthwhile, professionally, personally and not least for the Lebanese people; and the Irish had done well.

AT EASE

"If you think you understand the situation leaving this room, then you have not been briefed properly."

So read the sign above the operations room door at the Irish battalion headquarters. Humorous at first glance, it acknowledged the complexity of the Lebanese situation. As the Israeli army in the south moved towards the completion of their withdrawal, the power vacuum looked like being filled by Syria, a country which had established something close to a hegemony over Lebanon. Lebanon was a country destabilised by disruptive outside forces, the activities of Palestinian fighters, the two Israeli invasions and now the political and military intervention of Syria. Due to the complexity of the situation in which it found itself, Lebanon in a sense was a country which shouldn't have existed. The country's woes were due at least as much to the disagreements of the many factions within it. These divisions were deepening and becoming more violent.

Lebanon is much more than a geographical place, however. It is a unique society with its own intrinsic identity, social fabric, beliefs and values. The suffering Lebanese, a resilient and resourceful people, had survived against the odds. Despite the collapse of Lebanon into near anarchy and the appalling obstacles which remained in the way of any measures to prevent the country's total disintegration, peacekeeping was far from being a futile venture. Ultimately, it created an atmosphere where confidence-building and bridge-building allowed the diplomatic and political initiatives towards peace to take place. But then, these were a long way from succeeding.

In the south, some measure of stability had been provided by the presence of the United Nations' forces. As our replacements prepared to take up their dangerous, thankless and arduous peacekeeping duties, our good wishes were mingled with concern over the nature of their mandate and anxiety for their safety. It was plainly the intention of the Israelis to maintain an enlarged buffer zone in the south, patrolled by themselves and the Christian militia which they continued to arm and support. In the climate of inflamed Shia Muslim feelings, a local Christian-Muslim civil war could make the UN's position untenable.

But all this was for the new battalion. When the Israelis had completed their withdrawal to the new enclave line, the Irish battalion would find itself facing a new situation. Topographically, it was one which could be more easily defined, and without an Israeli army of occupation in the UN zone. Paradoxically, the mission could be more complicated. Prior to the Israeli army's invasions, the Irish battalion had tired to prevent Palestinian infiltrations passing north-to-south through its area of operations. Now, they would be faced with the prospect of living with the extremism of the Hezbullah faction of Shia men, some of whom operated from their home villages within the Irish battalion area. Having to exist with the fanaticism of some of the followers of Islamic Jihad would be a new undertaking, but it was for them to resolve the new realities on the ground. If the Irish were required to adapt, few were better equipped to do so. The Irish believed in "adaptability before experience", but they had the experience as well.

* * *

For us, no fairytale happy ending would coincide with our rotation home. We would leave the situation unresolved, with the Israeli army's withdrawal not quite completed, a village militia gang presence still in existence, and strife remaining prevalent in the area. We would have to reconcile ourselves to this: it is the nature of peacekeeping.

Notwithstanding its shortcomings, peacekeeping makes sense in the context of the brutality, the horror and the tragedy that was Lebanon. We had undoubtedly saved lives which would otherwise have been lost; we had protected an area which would otherwise have been undefended. By our actions and our sheer presence, we endured the pervading fear, lessening its grip on the population and bringing some semblance of stability to the area. We could and did feel proud that we had kept a fragile peace, albeit an armed one, and one shattered increasingly by confrontation and skirmishing. But it was a peace well worth defending all the same.

There could be no self-delusion, however. No one wins for long in Lebanon. We sometimes felt distraught, with a sense of emptiness when we were powerless to prevent some of the acts raging around us, and this, I suspect, troubled some of us. But that was the soldier in us talking. As soldiers, the chaotic nature of some of the peacekeeping situations to which we had been exposed was difficult to reconcile. As peacekeepers, there was a pragmatic, long-term logic to it all. Paradoxically, it was those same soldierly characteristics — teamwork, discipline, courage and leadership applied to the everyday operational problems — that made us effective peacekeepers.

Peacekeeping is not simply soldiering under a blue flag. It differs substantially from that which soldiers are normally called upon to do, but neither is it devoid of risk. Fortunately there were no Irish casualties during our time in Lebanon. The other battalions had not been so lucky. If it was our soldierly qualities which made us good peacekeepers who were drawn from an experienced professional army, it was our Irishness which made us natural peacekeepers. With no colonial past, we were, and were seen to be, impartial. In addition, our characteristic national personality was friendly, communicable, courteous and sensitive. The Irish had earned a reputation as capable, able peacekeepers and were well respected among the other contributing nations. We felt it an achievement to have maintained that reputation in very trying circumstances.

07 May 1985

The first week of May, with the handover to the new battalion completed, it was time for what remained of our battalion to rotate home. Chalk Three convoy, concentrated outside Irish battalion headquarters, had left our respective company areas an hour beforehand. It felt good to be going home. In truth we experienced a mixture of emotions: concern for all those coping with the situation; relief to be free of our responsibilities; most of all, sheer childish excitement at finally being homeward bound.

The exchange of banter, the wit, the good-natured humour were not tempered in any way by the continuing threat of village militia gangs to "hit up" one of the homeward rotation convoys. This threat of ambush was in retaliation for the injured militiamen which had occurred during a brief exchange of gunfire at the Irish battalion checkpoint four months previously. Despite his good recovery, we would not be allowed to leave Lebanon lightly. As the two previous convoys had rotated without incident, only one remained: us. An increased armoured presence placed within the convoy and additional leapfrogging by security parties secured the route in sectors and ensured our safe passage to UNIFIL headquarters in Naqoura. There, we rested for a while before a quick midnight crossing of the border into Northern Israel.

08 May 1985

Travelling south through the night, we arrived at Tel Aviv's Ben Gurion airport $4^1/_2$ hours later. After a further wait through the early morning dawn, we were positioned on the airport tarmac to begin boarding. It was lovely to see the shamrock on the tail fin of the specially chartered "big green bird" from Ireland. Our replacements had departed unseen by us and all was set for take-off. However, an air traffic controllers' strike in Greece delayed boarding and we took shelter from the sun's intense heat in the shade afforded by the massive wings of the Aer Lingus Jumbo jet until accommodation in the airport terminal building was eventually organised. There we endured a frustrating day-long wait for news of our departure. It eventually came, and the plane lifted off the runway in late afternoon to begin our five-hour flight to Dublin.

Despite the wait, the atmosphere on board was electric. An alcohol-free flight, no drink was necessary as we were intoxicated with thoughts of family, friends and home. The excitement was real, pure and infectious. Photographs of family members were being shown to the cabin crew who were obviously taken by our buoyant sense of how wonderful it was to be going home. Easing into the flight and beginning to relax, I switched my watch back two hours to Irish time, something I had waited six months to do, and tried to fall into a sound sleep.

The challenge of being a peacekeeper had taken a lot out of me. We had given our all in the curious chess game of confrontation. It presented an unrivalled opportunity to discover and develop the potential within you, something which you didn't know you had but which you hoped you did. We had all emerged stronger, more ready to take on the responsibility of command. Lebanon had forged strong bonds of friendship and camaraderie. The idea of overseas service no longer held us in awe. We had lived with the lack of home comforts and separation from family. We had felt the heightening tension, the sense of waiting for something to happen, and had experienced the devastating combination of danger and uncertainty. We had witnessed the grim horror and pointlessness of war, and knew the purposefulness and pride of peacekeeping. The sense of the occasion brought to mind the expression: "Every man thinks less of himself for never having been a soldier" — and we had been peacekeepers into the bargain.

Few people in Ireland have any military experience. Because of this, returning Irish peacekeepers are often, if discretely, asked what a war zone experience is like. We are all curious to know how we might react to it. Each platoon member had answered that question for himself, for it had undoubtedly been one of the toughest Lebanese tours in recent years. The luck of the Irish in not experiencing casualties was clearly expressed by a local villager when he commented that our God must be stronger than theirs as it was keeping the bullets away from us.

Camaraderie especially, but competence and confidence combined to make that sought-after reaction of physical courage less difficult to attain. Training, experience and adaptability, reinforced by the more elusive qualities of leadership, moral courage and character, were driven by a strong sense of purpose which made us equal to the demands. The situation was made chaotic by the Israeli defence forces' sanction of various brands of thuggery which supported a reign of terror inside Lebanon. In the south, they had pursued a vicious policy with their proxy killers when expanding their security zone. We had witnessed actual and attempted acts of violence and intimidation against the Lebanese villagers, offering our protection whenever possible against the brutality and cruelty of the Israeli-backed militias.

Peacekeeping had its limitations and consequently its frustrations, so feelings of fearfulness and helplessness could pervade upon one's consciousness. Having passed the critical initiations of soldiering and leadership, how had we faired in the crucial test of our own humanity? It was a question which could cause unease to the young minds of returning peacekeepers. Our peacekeeping role had challenged our comfortable militaristic mind-set and stereotypical assumptions. The Israelis had discovered that their might wasn't right, while the UN peacekeeping force had learned that being right was not necessarily might.

Peacekeepers find their task more challenging than war, as the initiative is always with the aggressor. Peacekeeping is a difficult role for soldiers and is much less clear-cut than war. Conflict is an upsetting experience, not least for the local inhabitants. Most of all, I felt a distinct pride in the platoon's performance, mixed with anxiety for the plight of the people. This sadness was combined with much relief to be going home. I wondered whether, one day, I would be back.

* * *

We touched down, exhausted but elated, on Dublin airport runway two-four and our delight was expressed by a huge roar the instant the Jumbo touched down. It was a roar much appreciated by the aircraft's captain who, in keeping with the spirit of things, thanked us for flying Aer Lingus and hoped we would do so again.

* * *

"Hurry up and wait" is a saying well known to all soldiers, and we would have to wait for our baggage to be unloaded, then spot-checked by Customs before proceeding from the airport. The essential peacekeeping qualities of inexhaustible patience and energy were now at a low ebb as all were anxious to be reunited with their families. Many among us had still to travel to destinations such as Cork and Donegal.

Over two hours later, we entered the French Renaissance structure of McKee Barracks, its magnificent red-bricked buildings complete with high chimneys, steeply pitched roofs, gables, and high dormer windows. Built in a mixture of French château, Elizabethan, Queen Anne and Tudor styles, the barracks' unique design gave rise to the myth that its plans were intended for India, not Ireland. Delight, jubilation and excitement brought the square to life as the convoy swept through the gate, completing the last leg of what had been an exhausting journey from the Middle East. There, patiently waiting well into the early May night, were members of our families. A spontaneous scene erupted with the sheer thrill of the happy reunions giving way to numerous hugs and many kisses. Shrieks of "Daddy! Daddy!" echoed as children with outstretched arms ran towards weary soldiers laden down by heavy bags. Tired, tanned and dressed in our bright-coloured uniforms, we could only search for words to describe our sense of relief at being back to familiar, peaceful territory and family. The joy-filled tears which dominated the reunions rendered any carefully turned expression of happiness redundant. It had been a fascinating six-month journey from the beginning. Homecoming had made it complete.

* * *

I was very much at peace with myself. There was nothing left to prove. I was glad to be home. It was then that I caught sight of the darkened, faceless windows of the now-silent briefing room where I had attended the officer briefing session seven months previously. I became aware of a certain tinge of restlessness and I had to wonder whether Lebanon was beginning to weave its peculiar type of magic. In spite of myself, I began to think... while in no immediate hurry to return... would the next trip be any different?

POSTSCRIPT

October 2001

Ironically, part of the extraordinariness of the overseas journey is the return to Ireland. In South Lebanon, we bore witness to conflict close-up, with events sometimes placing us in the centre of chaos. We had lived through these shared experiences: the remoteness, the tension, the responsibility, sometimes the fear. Ireland is a blissful world apart, largely unmoved by Middle Eastern events. The resultant gulf between the recent on-ground realities, the intensity of the confrontations, and the indifference, albeit unconscious, of those back home can make homecoming difficult. Returning Irish peacekeepers are suddenly in a very different world and experience a stark change in pace. Neither is this change entirely one-sided, for those who had adjusted to our absence are now having to readjust to our presence. For some it can mean feeling, however briefly, like an intruder in your own home. Time soon restores the equilibrium and allows life's rhythms to continue.

Time too grants a perspective on the time spent in Lebanon. It affords an overall appraisal of the Irish presence there. Each platoon's involvement is in turn but a part of each Irish battalion's peacekeeping efforts. The Irish battalion was one of the six making up the greater part of Lebanon's UN Peacekeeping Force. An international reservoir of goodwill sustained this UN operation in South Lebanon.

The Irish arrived in Lebanon in June 1978 with an already high reputation. Previous UN service in the Congo and Cyprus, with involvement in security operations at home, meant they were among the best equipped, most mobile and highly experienced units in the UNIFIL mission.

The Irish knew all too well that it was going to be a difficult mission. When attempting to keep the peace, they knew they would have to bear witness to and report on what was really happening in the war in South Lebanon: the brutalities, horror, pain and death. They knew they were going to face risks.

The common-sense approach of forty-seven successive Irish battalions over twenty-three years, their sensitive integration and their consistent adaptation to the evolving operational environment meant they were able to provide a stablising presence in the midst of the various militias, contributing towards the hard-won stability of South Lebanon. Forty-four Irish soldiers had died in Lebanon. One, Private Kevin Joyce, remains missing.

The continuing conflict in South Lebanon placed great demands on defence force personnel and resources throughout these years of involvement. It meant responding to periods of tremendous change; re-organisation; re-equipment; and especially the emergence of new and complex multi-faceted overseas missions.

On 10 May 2001, Lieutenant Colonel Dave Ashe, Officer Commanding Eighty-Eighth Irish Battalion, handed over command of the Irish battalion area in Lebanon to Lieutenant Colonel Gerry Hegarty, Officer Commanding Eighty-Ninth Irish Battalion. The last hand-over parade was formed up under the direction of their respective battalion sergeants-major. The Eighty-eighth Battalion handed over the area of operations with new positions unfamiliar to previous battalions: Bin Jbaul, Safff Al Hawa and Blinda. The local Lebanese were visibly disappointed that this would be the last Irish battalion to serve in UNIFIL, and all sections of the community stated that when six months had elapsed, it would be hard to say good-bye to friends of twenty-three years. It was the intention of the last Irish battalion to build on work carried out by its predecessors. At the end of their tour, the Irish withdrew with dignity from South Lebanon, their task completed.

UNIFIL had been the one constant in the lives of the people of South Lebanon for more than two decades. "Irish Batt" has been the one constant battalion of UNIFIL, and our presence made a difference. Performing valuable service by protecting the villages of this region from the activities of the Israeli-backed militia has been vital in sustaining hope for the Lebanese.

The UNIFIL mission was difficult. In order to keep the peace, you must have it first, and the UN force in South Lebanon was often criticised for not achieving anything. UNIFIL, however, was neither a combat nor a diplomatic agency. Instead, it could be best described as a conflict-control presence whose strength was in holding ground and negotiating. The Irish had been particularly good at this. Their success may be best measured by imagining what would have happened if they weren't there, if they hadn't maintained their impartiality and been even-handed. This situation had been facilitated by the stabilising influence of UNIFIL, with Irish Batt providing a degree of normalisation for the people in their area. Realising this meant that many Irish soldiers continued to serve there as peacekeepers.

I, too, returned and serve further peacekeeping tours in Lebanon, each different from the previous. Warfare is as old as history, while peacekeeping is a modern phenomenon. The Irish have been among the pathfinders and have established a worthy tradition and an envied international reputation. Irish peacekeepers are considered to be some of the world's most acceptable. They are drawn from a professional army. Ireland is a neutral country which is non-aligned and was never a colonial power. The ethos of the Irish soldier, based on experience gained at home, is to contain violence in a community rather than to exacerbate it. Irish soldiers also have a unique talent for earning the trust and confidence of the conflicting parties and the local population. They have the ability to defuse potentially explosive situations through tact, dialogue and humour.

From 1960 to the present day, the Irish defence forces have provided an armed contingent to the UN, except during the period May 1974 to May 1978. These contingents normally comprised an infantry battalion of approximately 600 personnel or an infantry group of 400.

This significant contribution has not been without cost, and it is important to remember the forty-five Irish soldiers who died in the cause of peace. Peace should be safe, secure and strong, a peace that people can live with. Sixteen years after our platoon's return from South Lebanon, and twenty-three years since Irish peacekeepers first deployed there, it appears as if such a peace may come about. The Israeli withdrawal back to their original international border has led to the permanent disappearance of the Israeli-backed militia from the landscape of the UN area of operations. The situation in the former Israeli-controlled area of South Lebanon has stabilised. For Irish Batt, there is peace in their area of South Lebanon. After twenty-three years of Israeli occupation, the guns are finally silent: a peacekeeper's victory. For the individual platoon member, peacekeeping is a parochial, localised experience which is almost impossible to relate. Nevertheless, I have learned that it is the individual on-ground peacekeeper who wins the peace.

* * *

For now, the Lebanese war has ceased. The focus of the Israeli-Palestinian conflict has changed stage to within Israel itself. The "Intafada" has descended into near anarchy. The region's wrath of ages continues to erupt and the world wonders whether Jerusalem can be a capital for Jew and Palestinian alike or whether this is war-without-end.

Meanwhile, an armed Irish contingent prepares to return to the continent of Africa, to be deployed along the Ethiopian-Eritrean border. It was to Africa, the Congo, that the first armed Irish contingent was deployed over forty years ago. Currently, armed Irish peacekeepers are serving the cause of peace in the troubled Balkans. For some people around the world, the UN flag has become as familiar as their own. Irish peacekeepers have contributed significantly — and will continue to contribute — in giving it credibility.